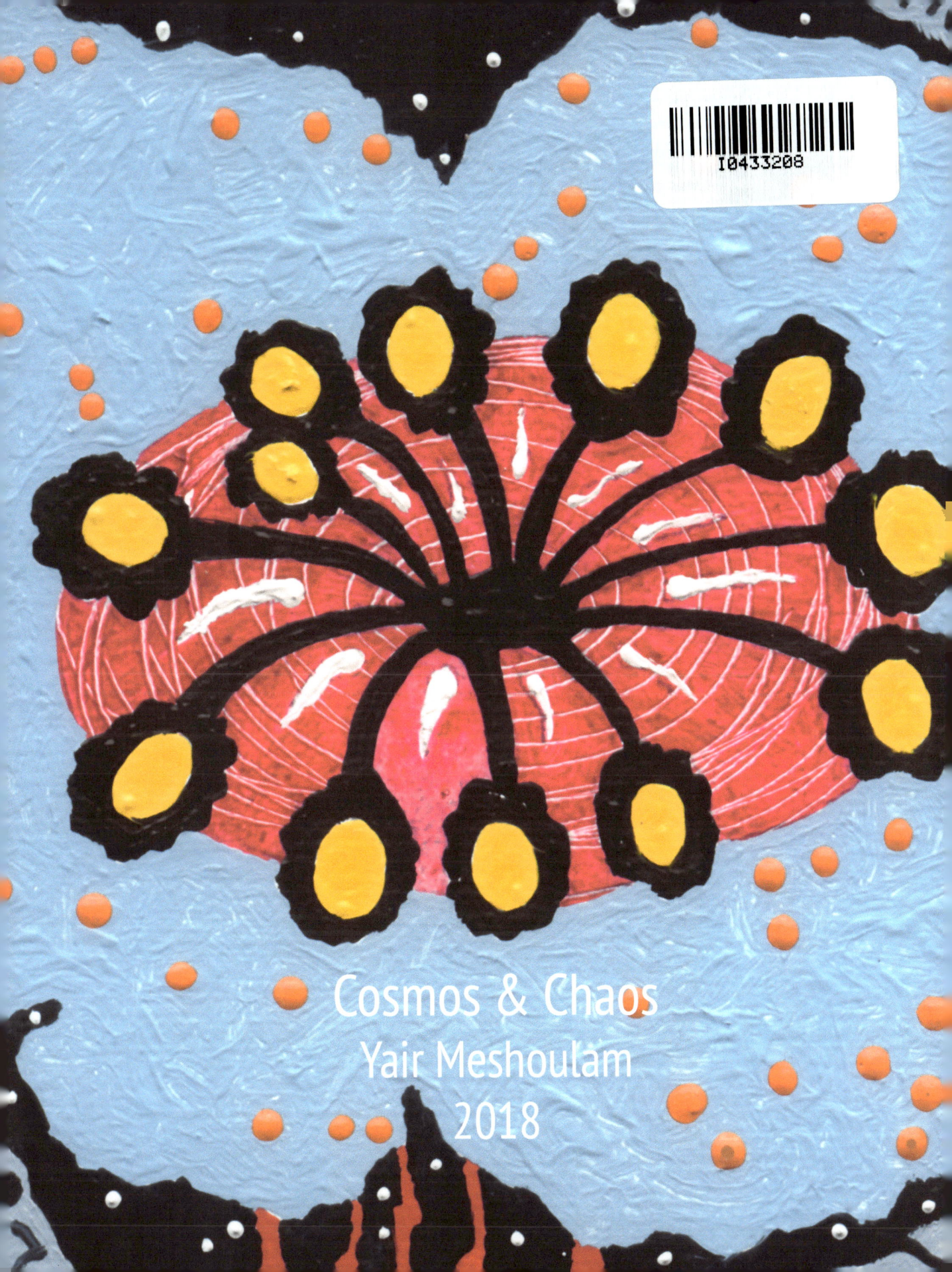

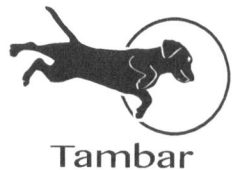
Tambar

June 2019

Paperback ISBN: 978-1-910133-17-0

Tambar Arts Ltd
e-mail: contact@tambar.co.uk
Reg. No. 03937329
www.tambar.co.uk

Copyright © Yair Meshoulam 2019 as the author of the article "Cosmos and Chaos" and all Artworks
Copyright © Lily Fürstenow 2019 as the author of the article "Creativity Begins"
Copyright © Keith Harrison-Broninski 2019 as the author of the article "Cosmos, Chaos and Improvisation"
Copyright © Jean Boulton 2019 as the author of the article "Political Conciousness"
Copyright © Robert Silman 2019 as the author of the article "Benign Catastrophe"

Book Design Dylan Martin www.friedbanana.co.uk

All rights reserved. No part of this publication may be reproduced, stored in or introduced into a retrieval system, or transmitted, in any form, or by any means (electronic, mechanical, photocopying, recording or otherwise) without the prior written permission of the publisher. Any person who does any unauthorized act in relation to this publication may be liable to criminal prosecution and civil claims for damages

A CIP catalogue record for this book is available from the British Library

This book is sold subject to the condition that it shall not, by way of trade or otherwise, be lent, resold, hired out, or otherwise circulated without the publisher's prior consent in any form of binding or cover other than that in which it is published and without a similar condition, including this condition, being imposed on the subsequent purchaser.

Contents

1   Cosmos and Chaos *Yair Meshoulam*   4
2   Contributions from friends   57
3   Index of artworks   77
4   Biographies   85

As I woke up and looked out
of the window

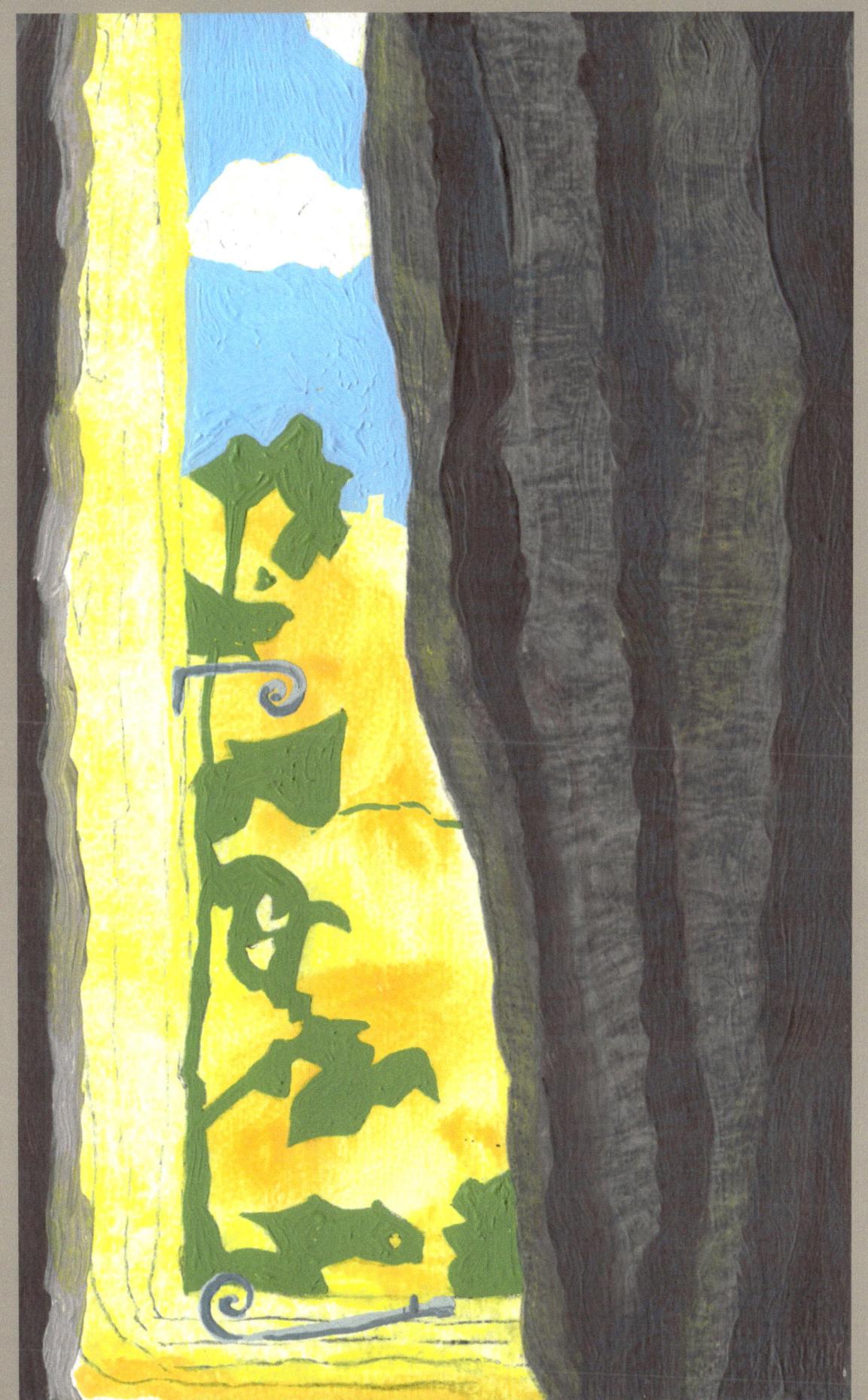

I realised that I was still in the middle of a dream
About a Brain-flower sprouting out of an egg implanted
In the skull of my dead ancestors
As I felt the texture of consciousness
Run across my hand.

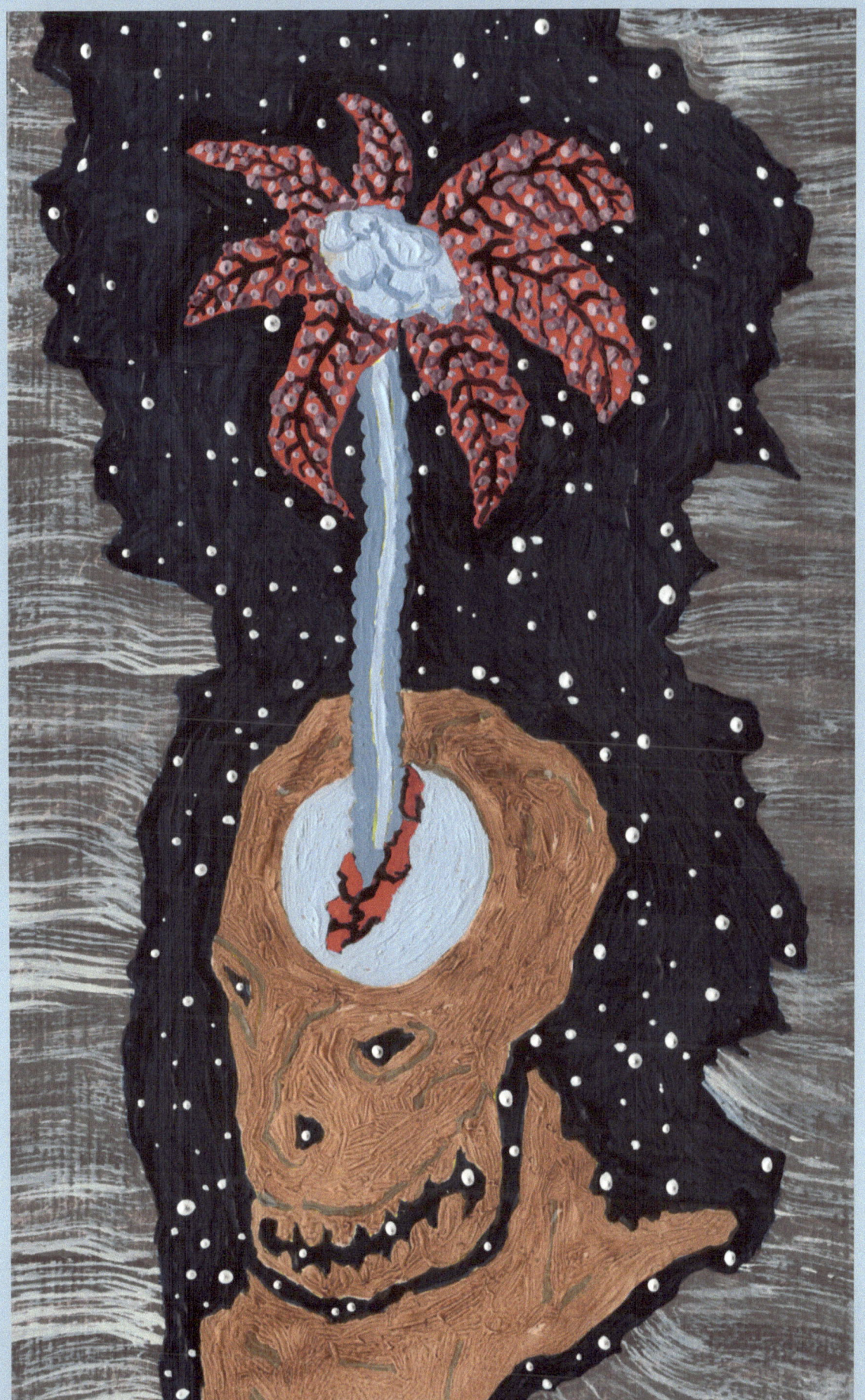

It hadn't been that long since the last solar eclipse had crossed America.

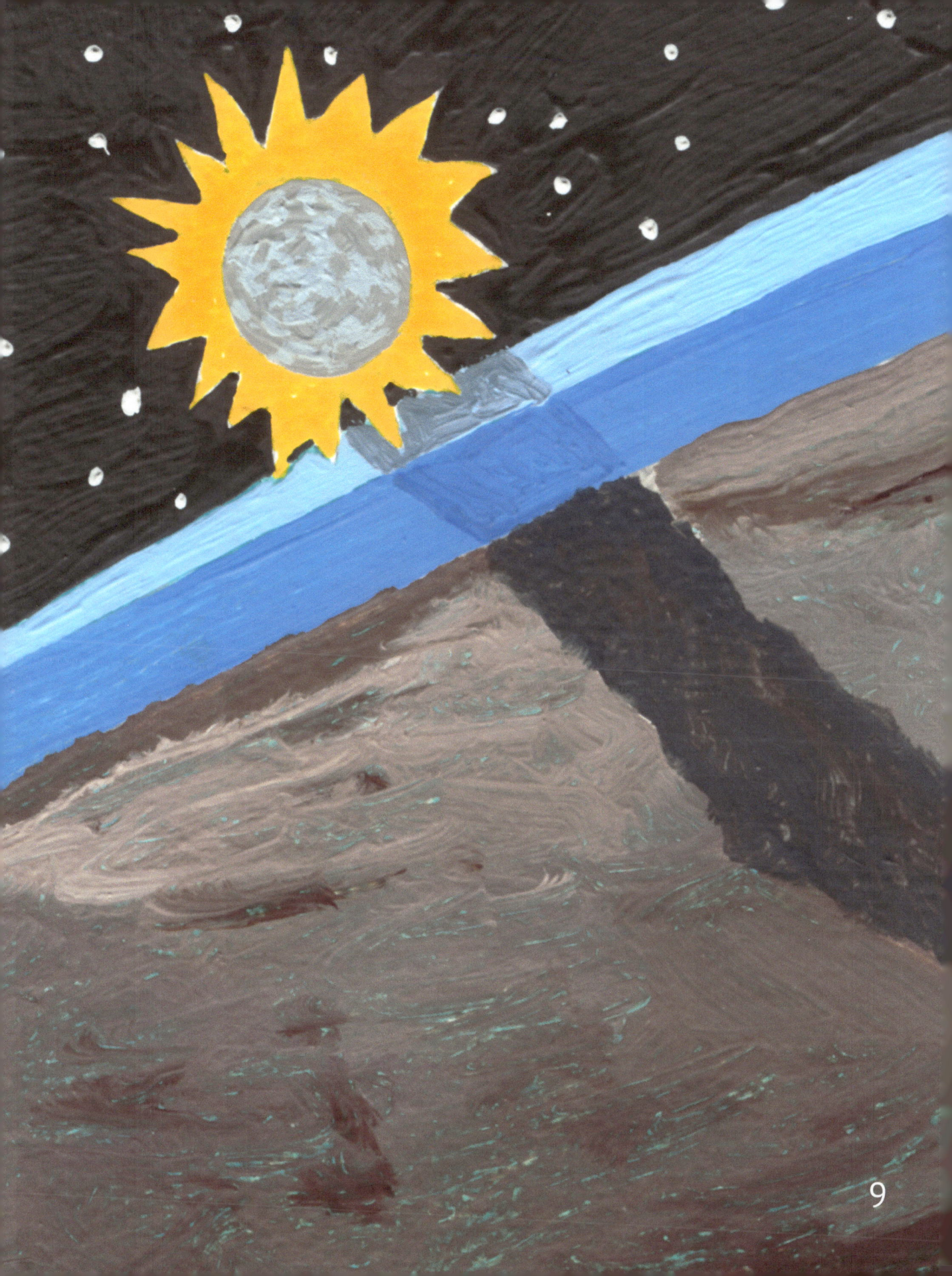

Even though the plants remained fixed to the ground

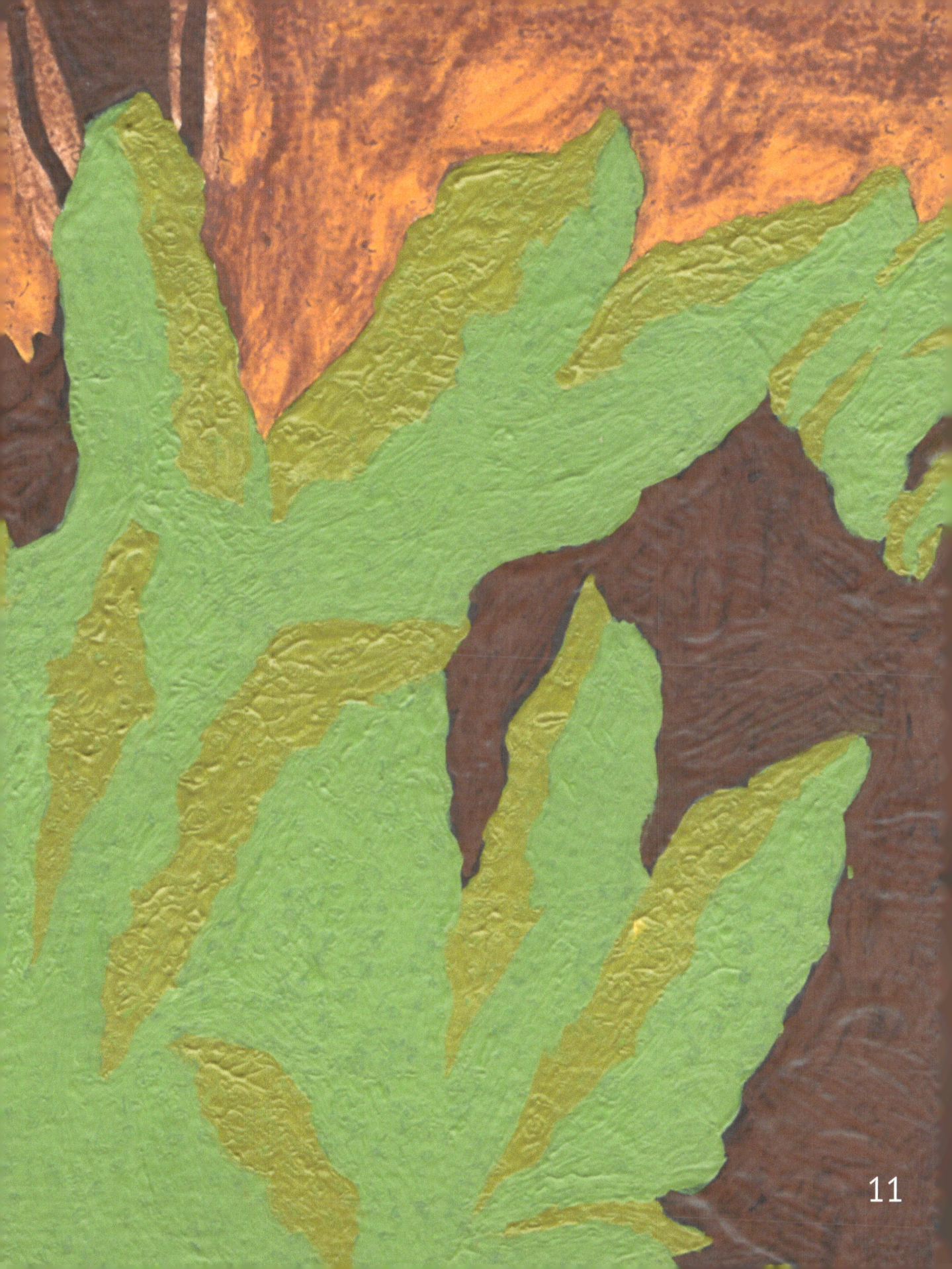

The cloud of cerebral data floated overhead,

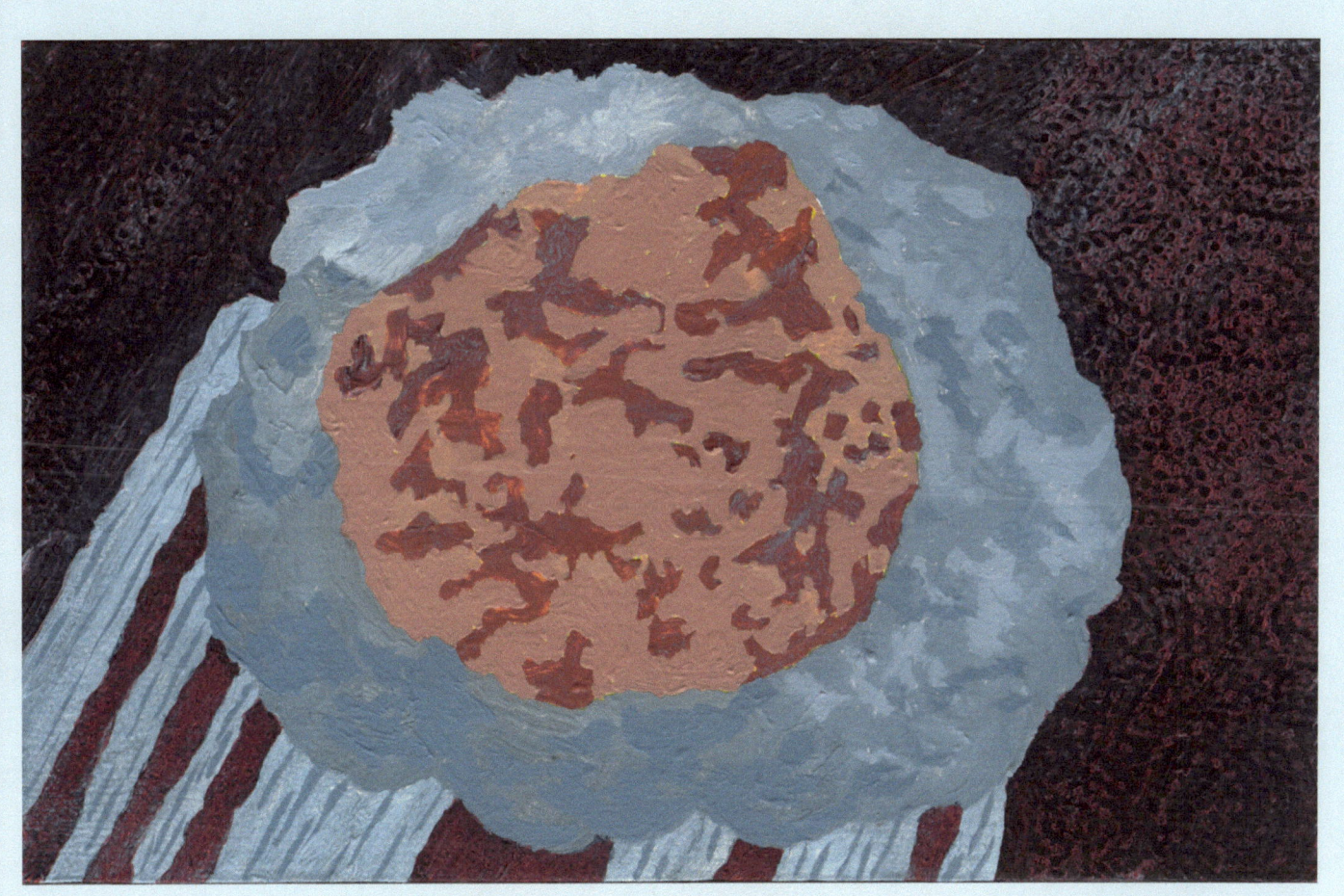

And on its reverse the Flower of Chaos

Tipped the saturation point to overflow.

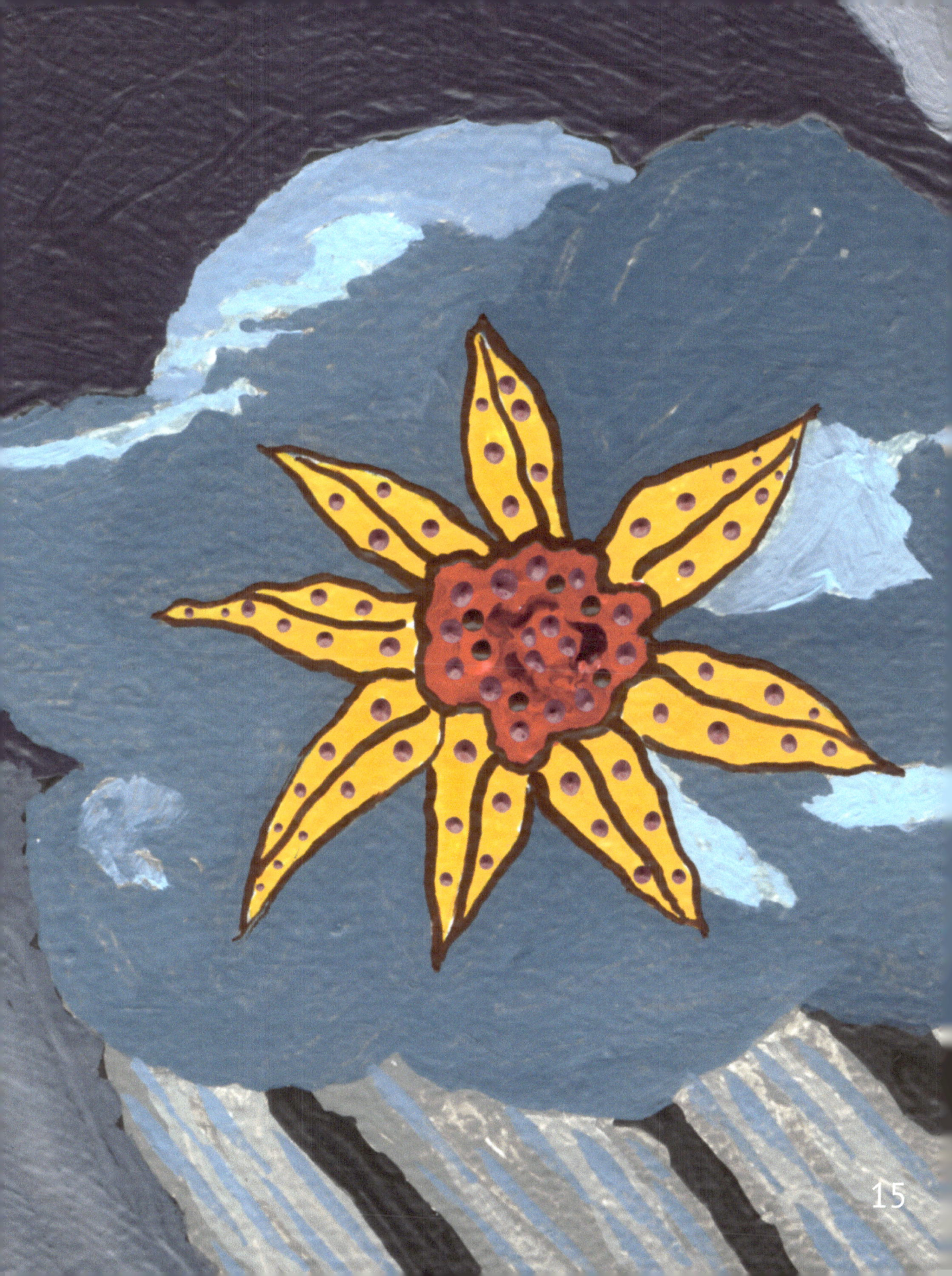

Not long after, the photos from Saturn
were beamed back to Earth,
Like a Roman god reversing the phone charges.

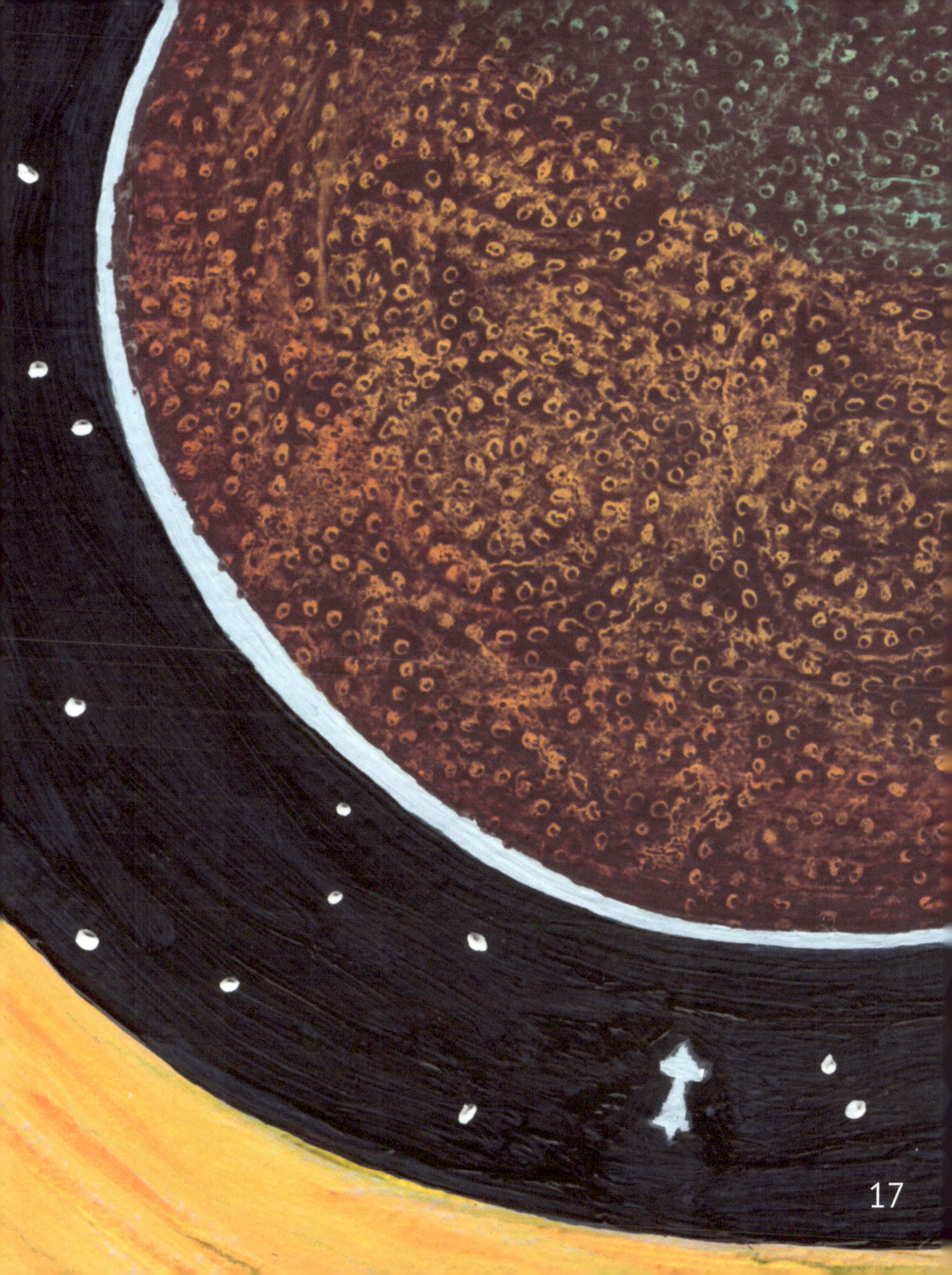

Meanwhile,
As I stood on the Dorset cliff beach
Staring out at Durdle Door,
The birds began to circle,

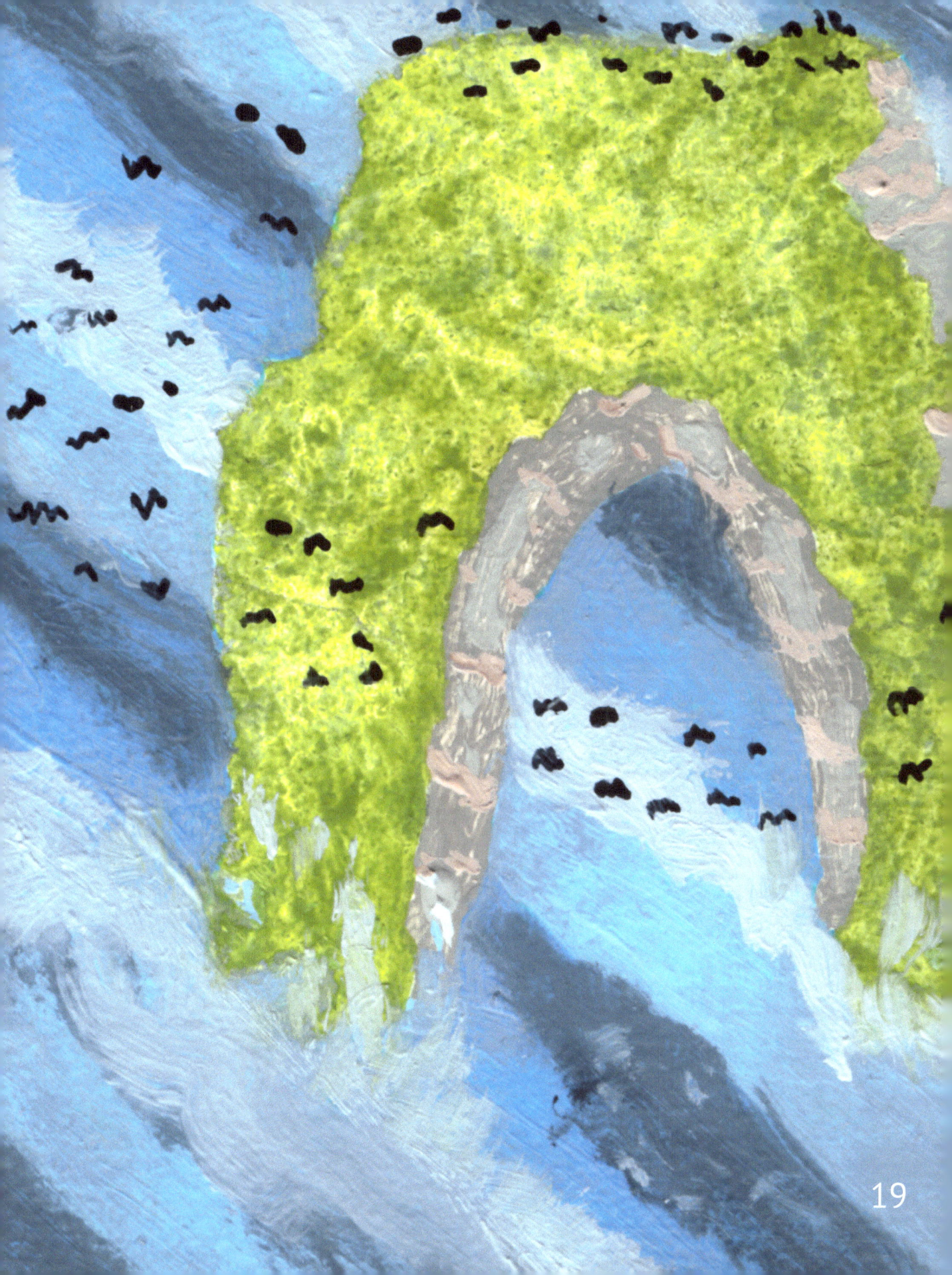

And as the Moon descended through the night sky,
And the light caressed the surface of Gaia,

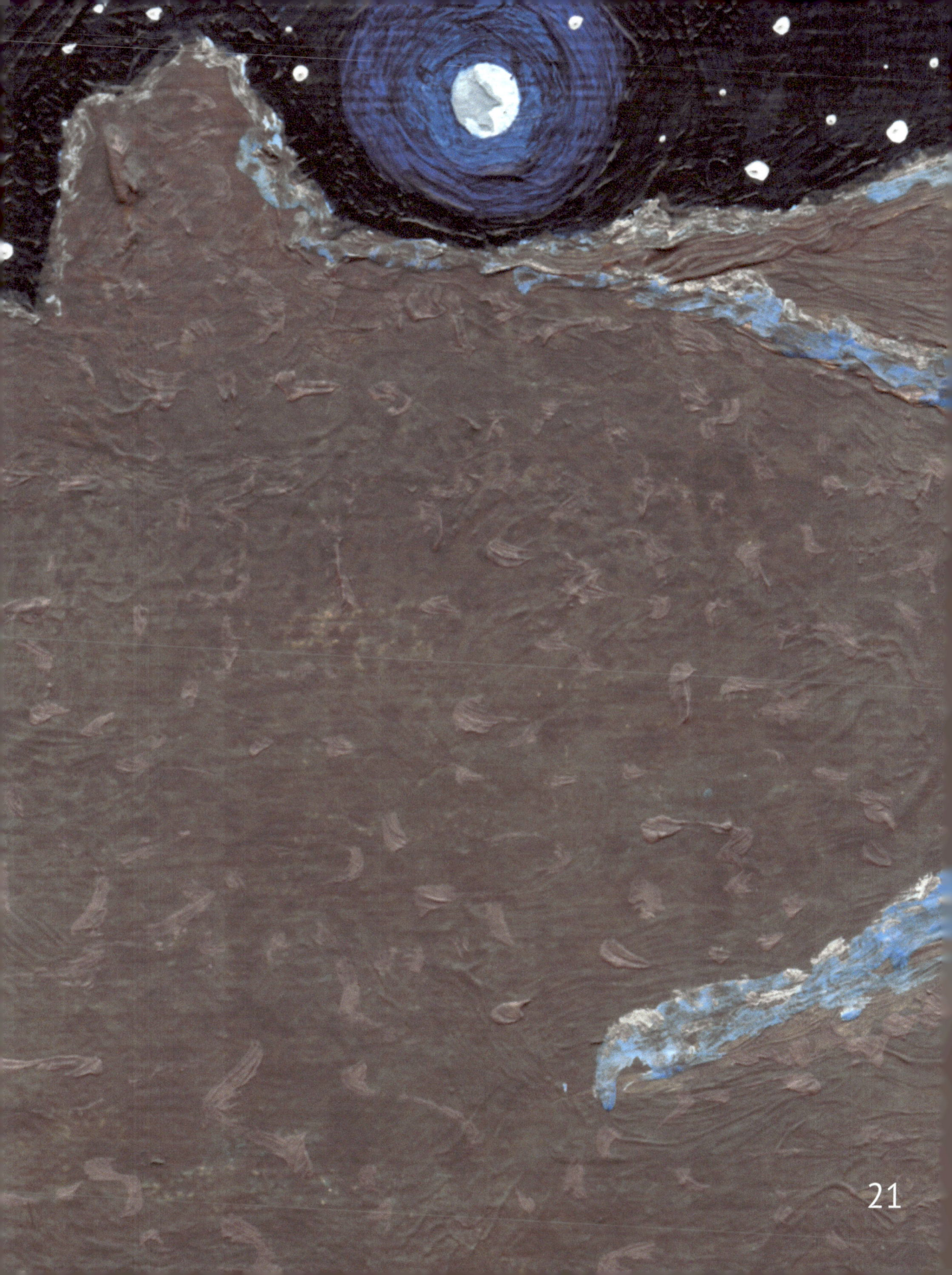

Lightning struck the house of the contained body,

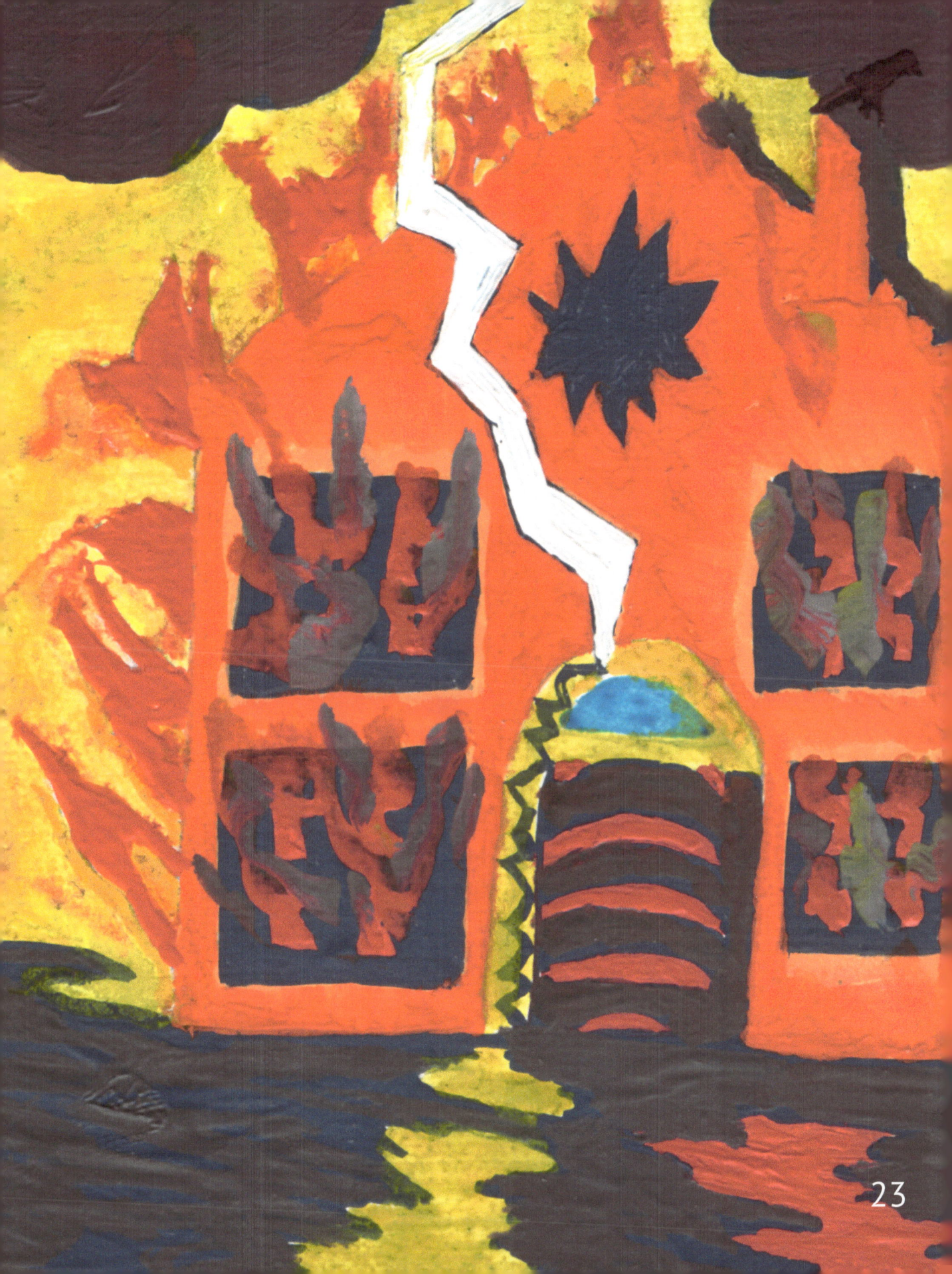

The data soul bird flew from its chimney,

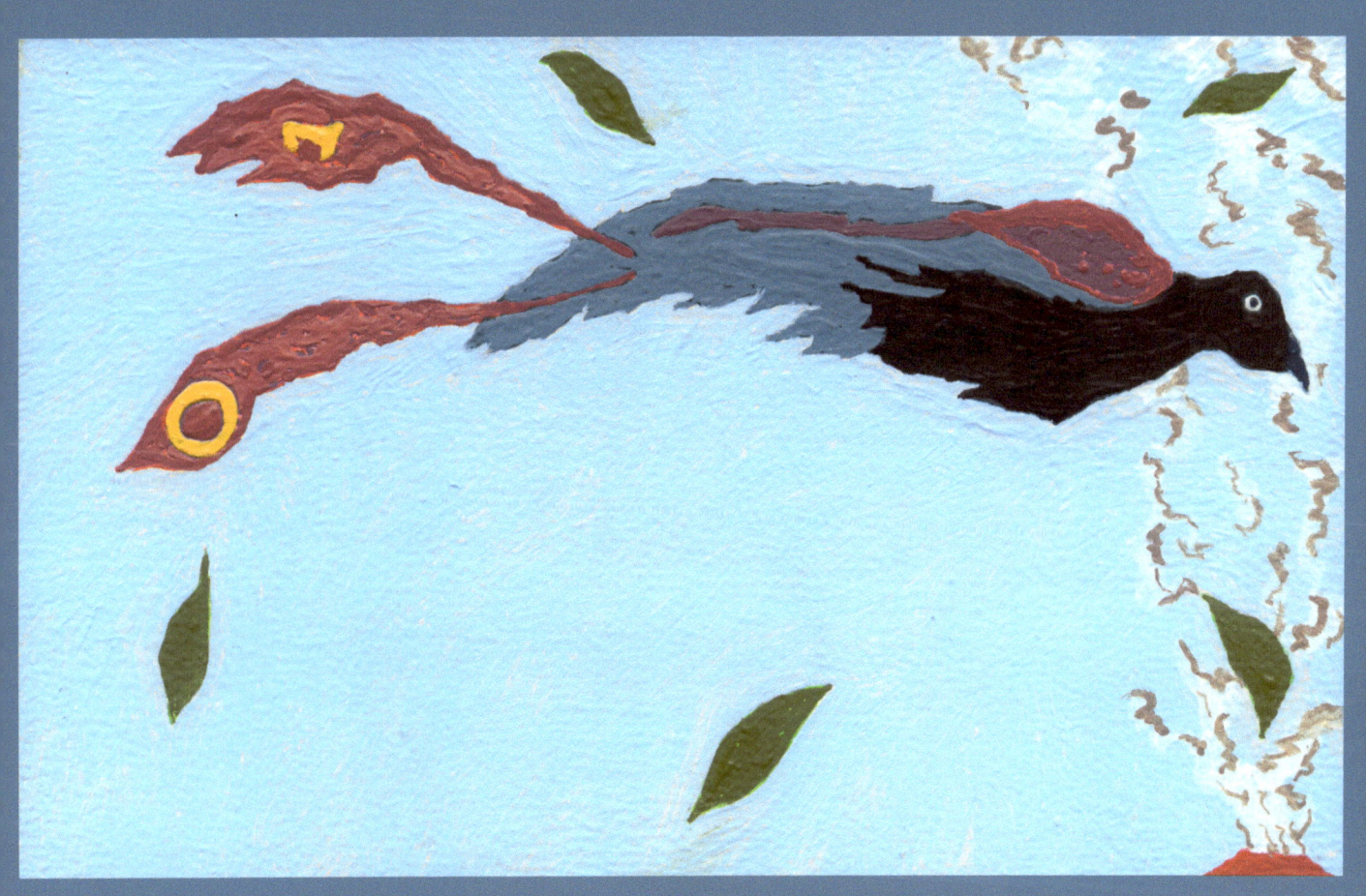

And saw, far in the distance,
The magma anger of the Volcano-god erupting.

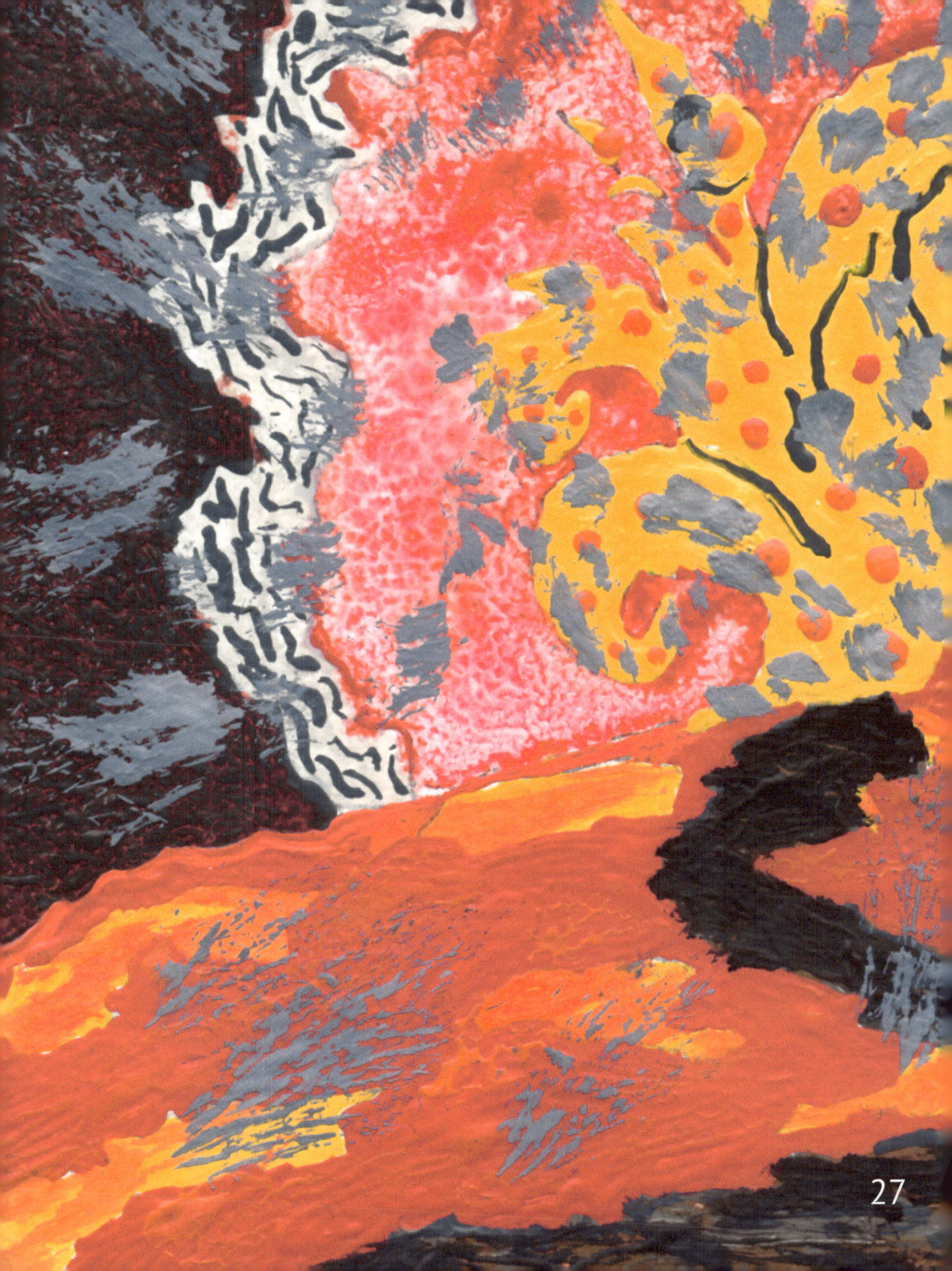

My heart remained beating but still,

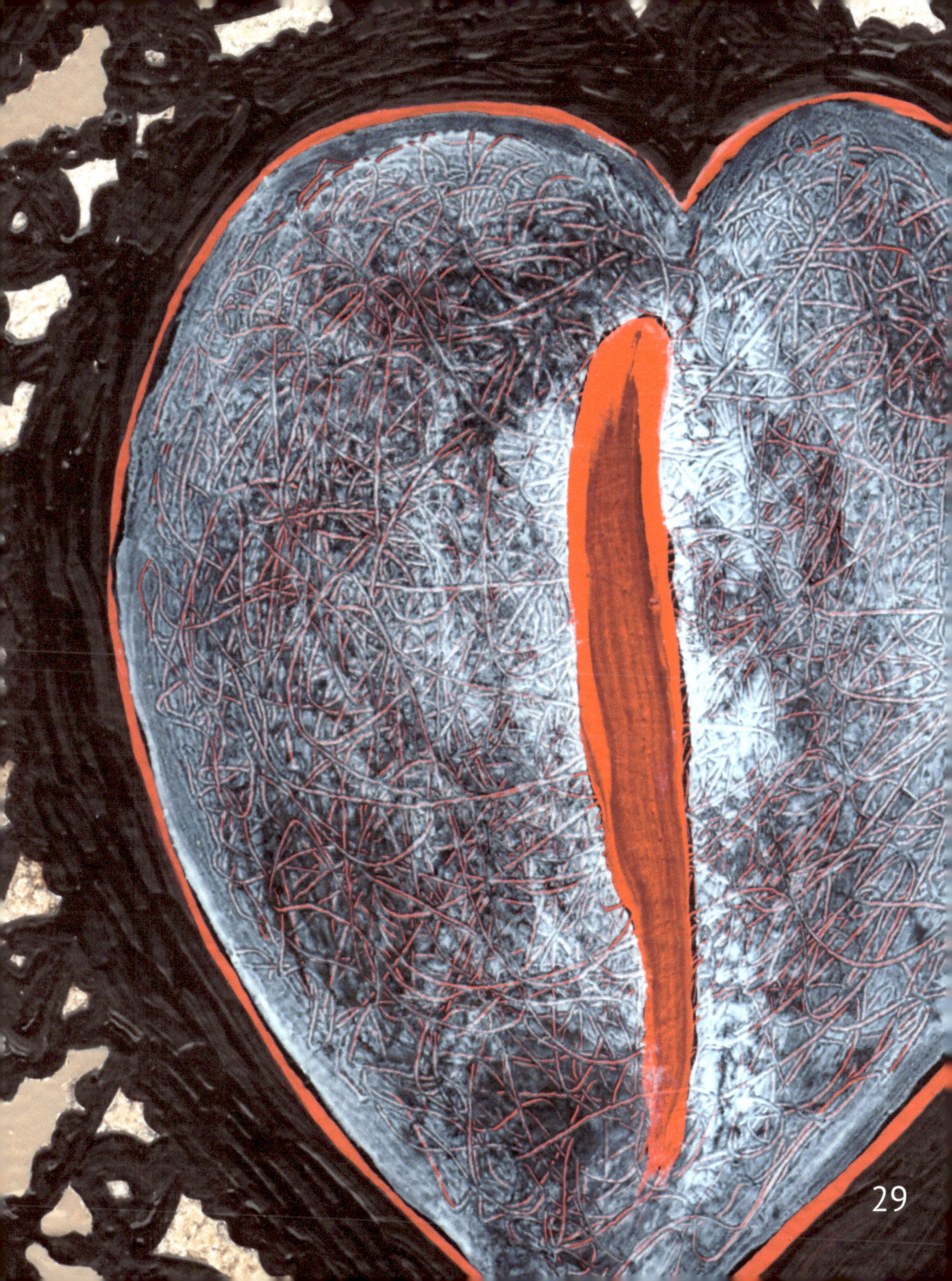

And sent a message to instruct
The fern of Action to unfurl

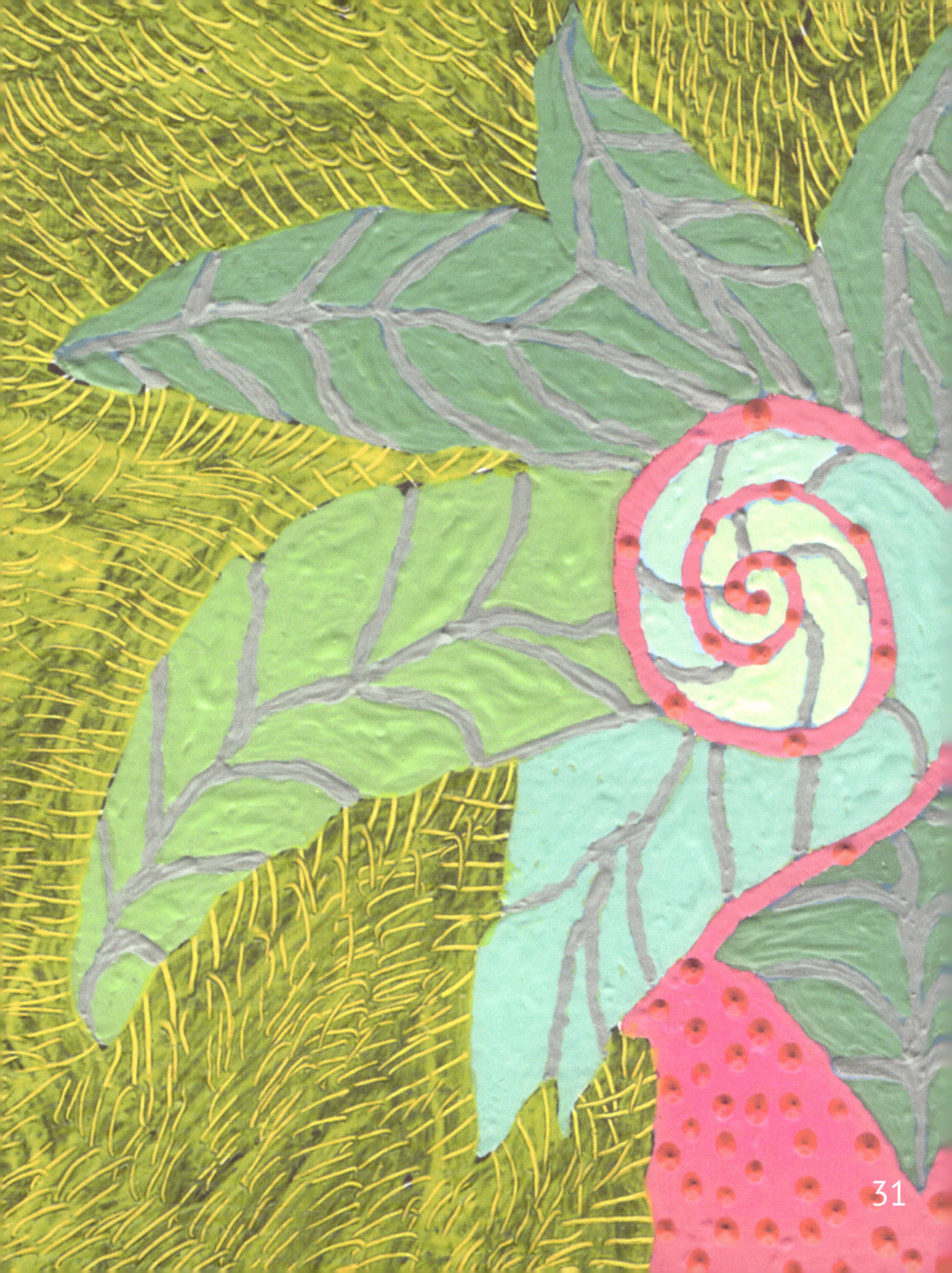

In the spiral pattern of the Cosmos

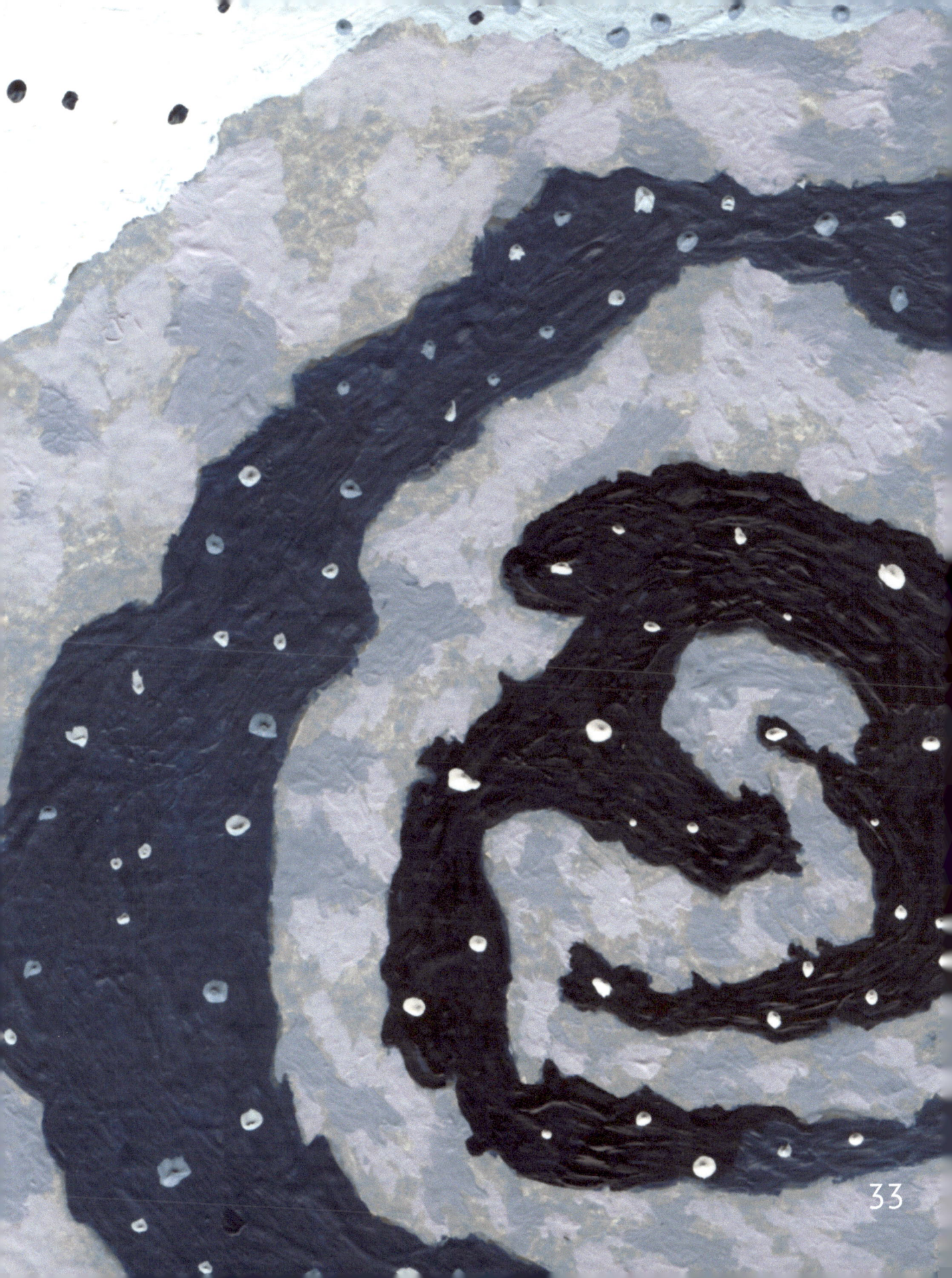

And the wave patterns of the seas of tranquility

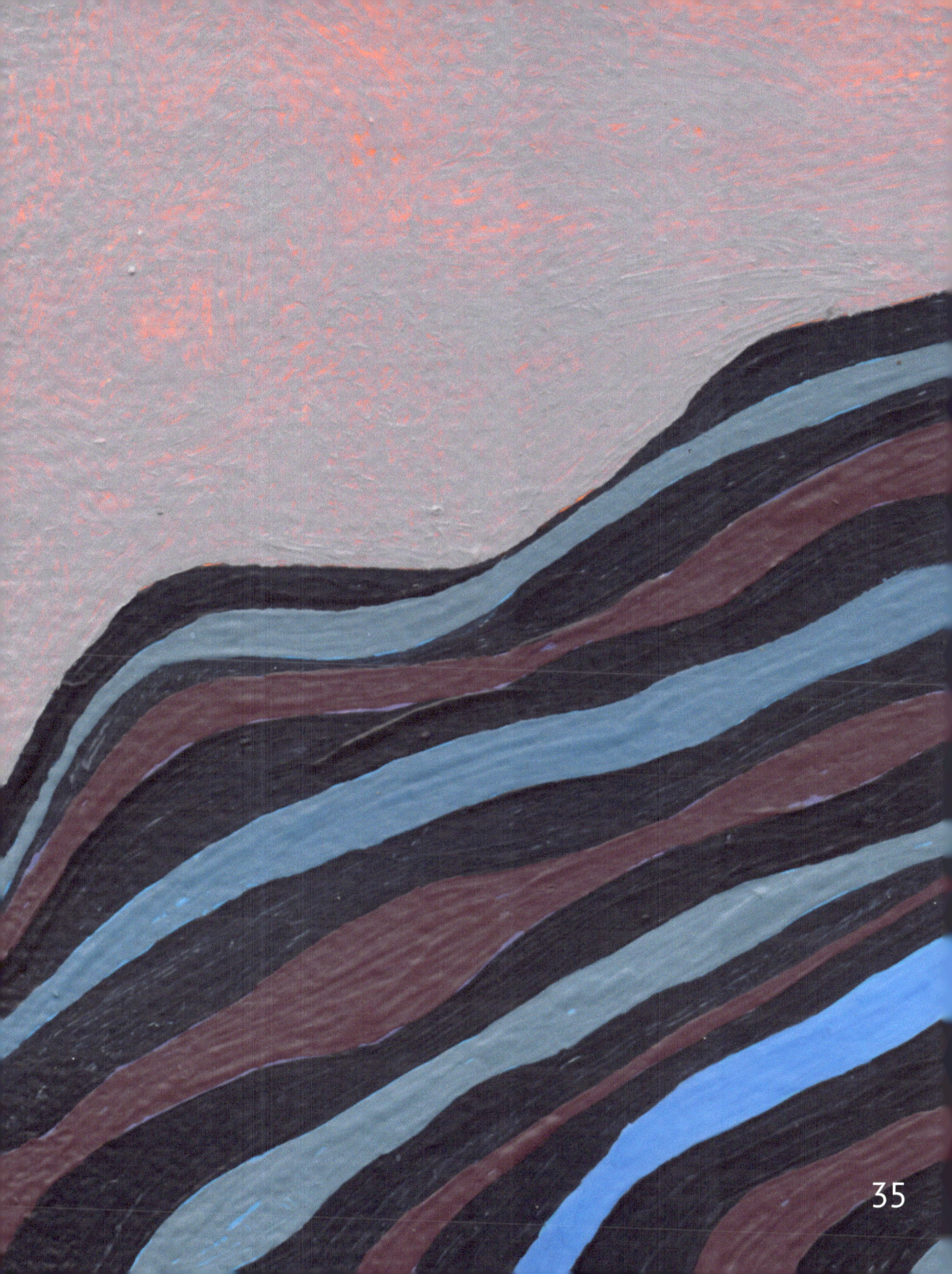

Beyond the seeming chaos of randomness, of undetected pattern.

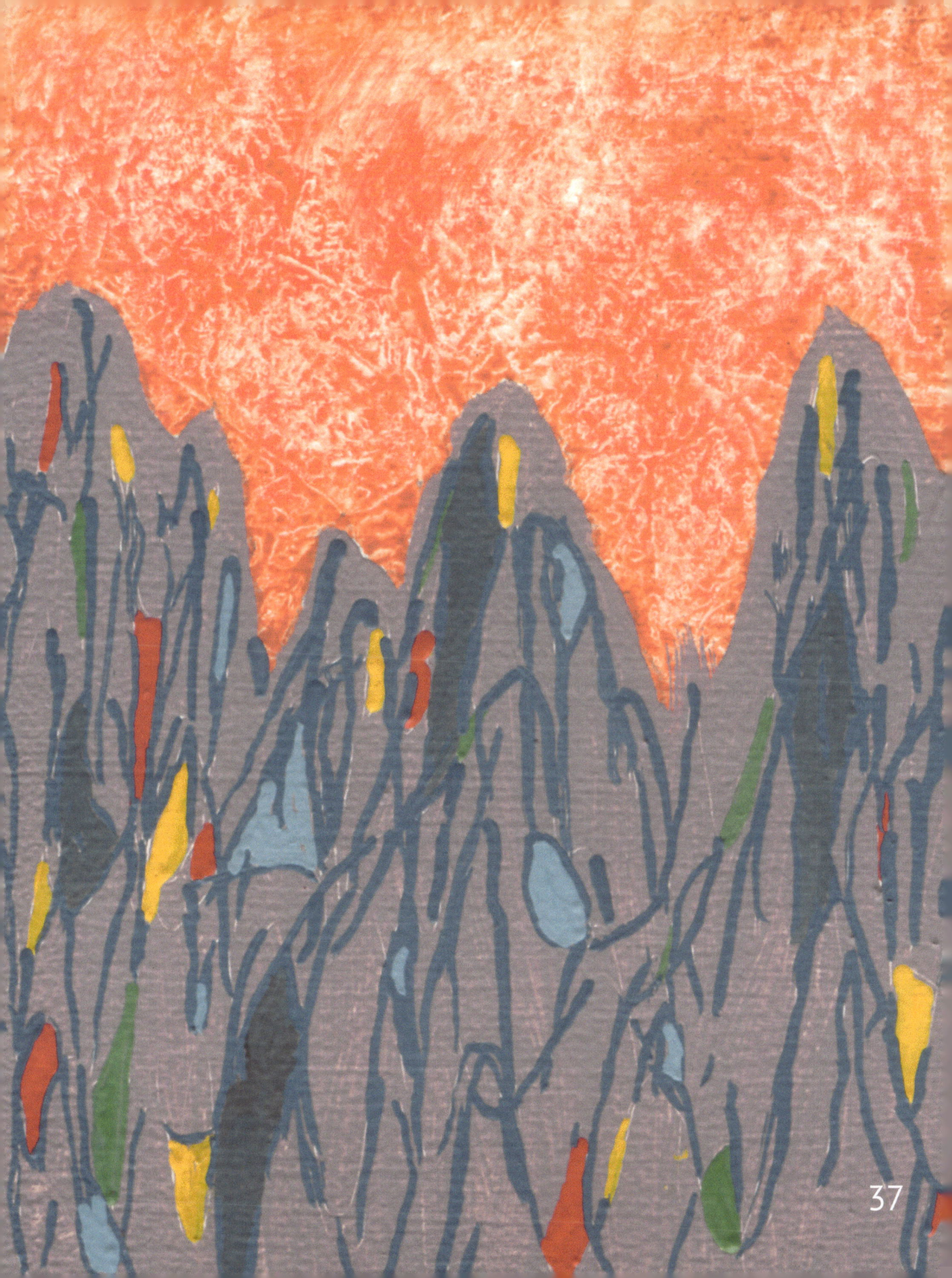

But from afar:
　　The Moon and Earth seemed
　　So purposeful;

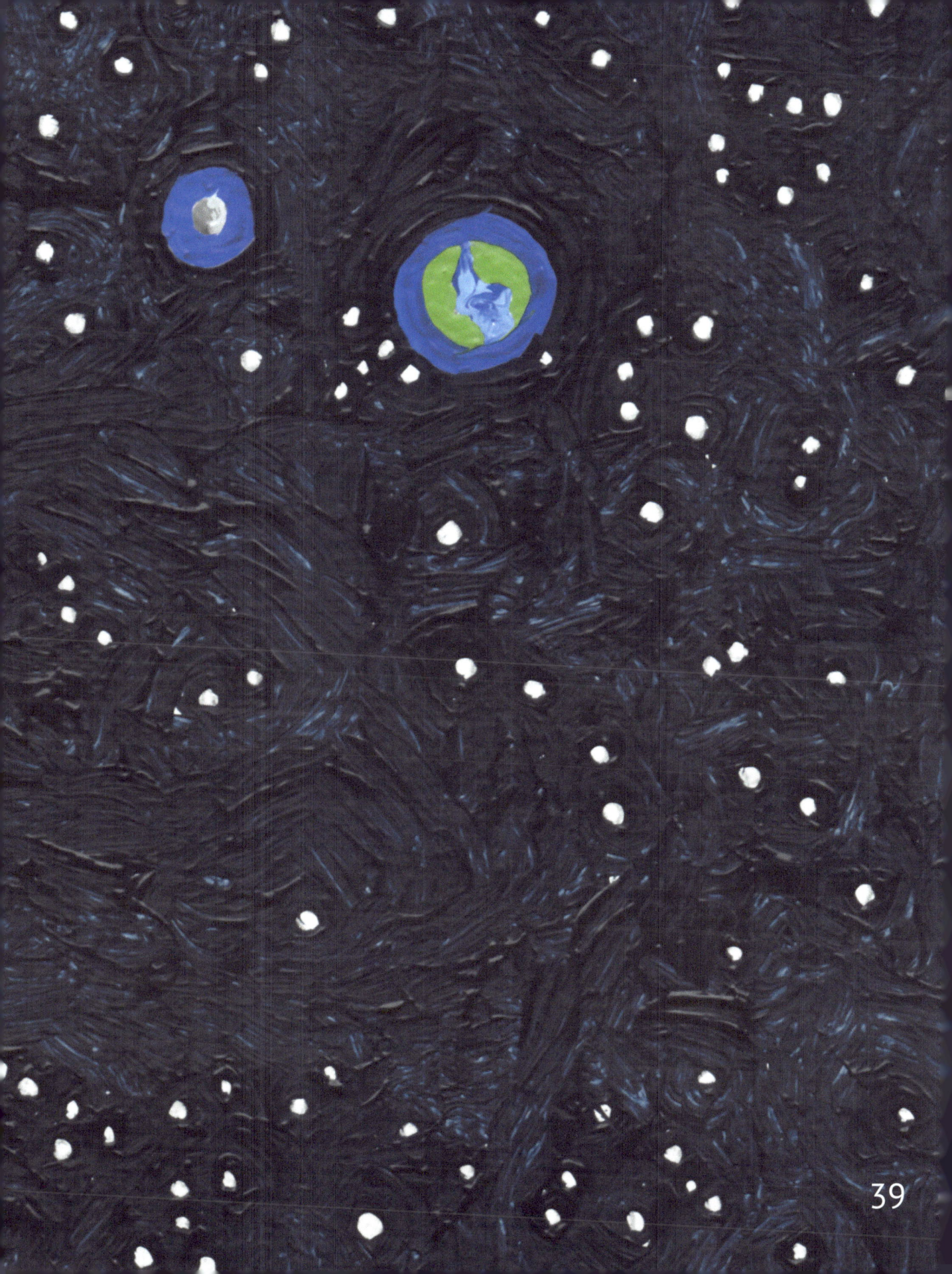

The Lilies so intent;

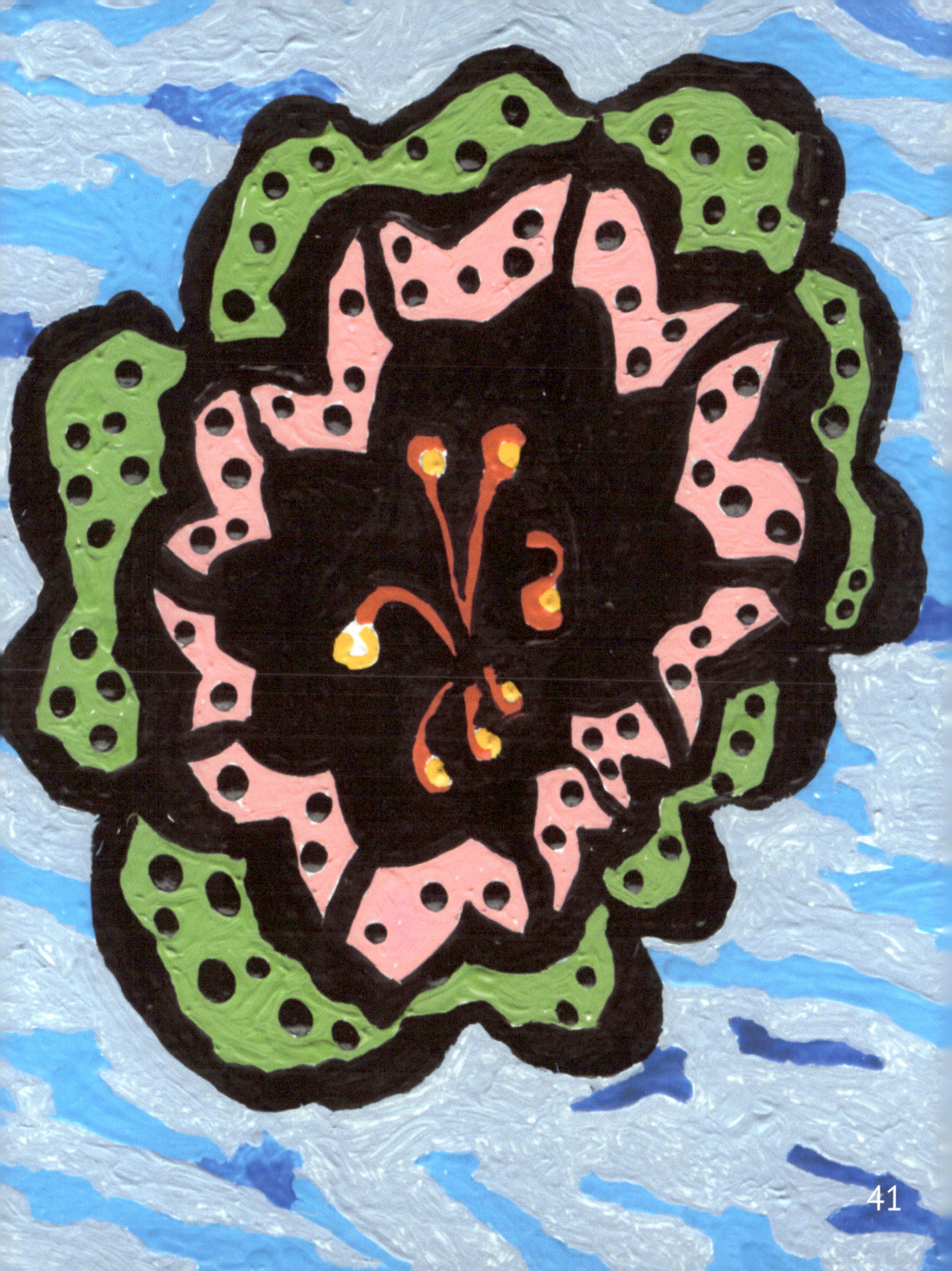

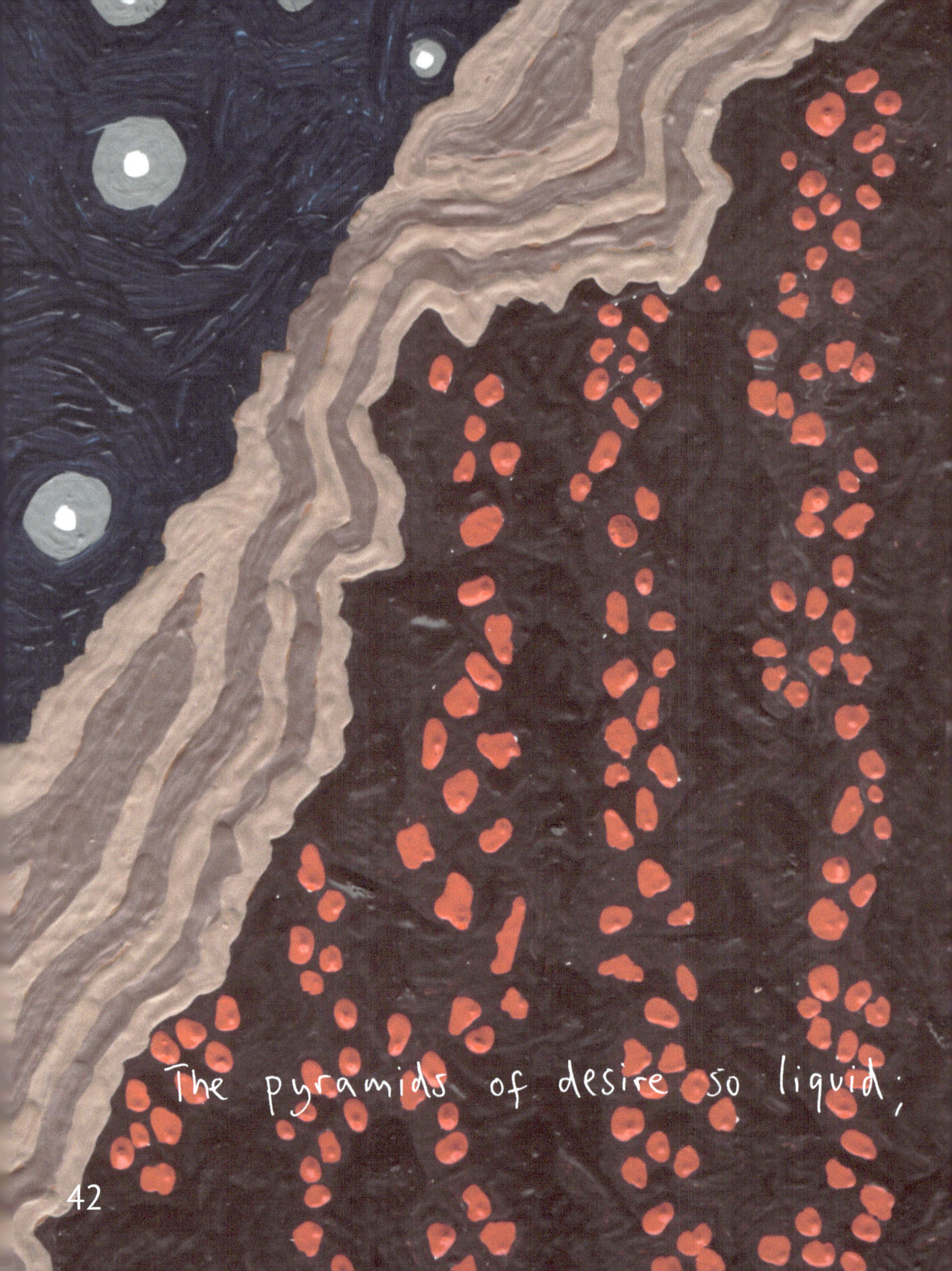
The pyramids of desire so liquid;

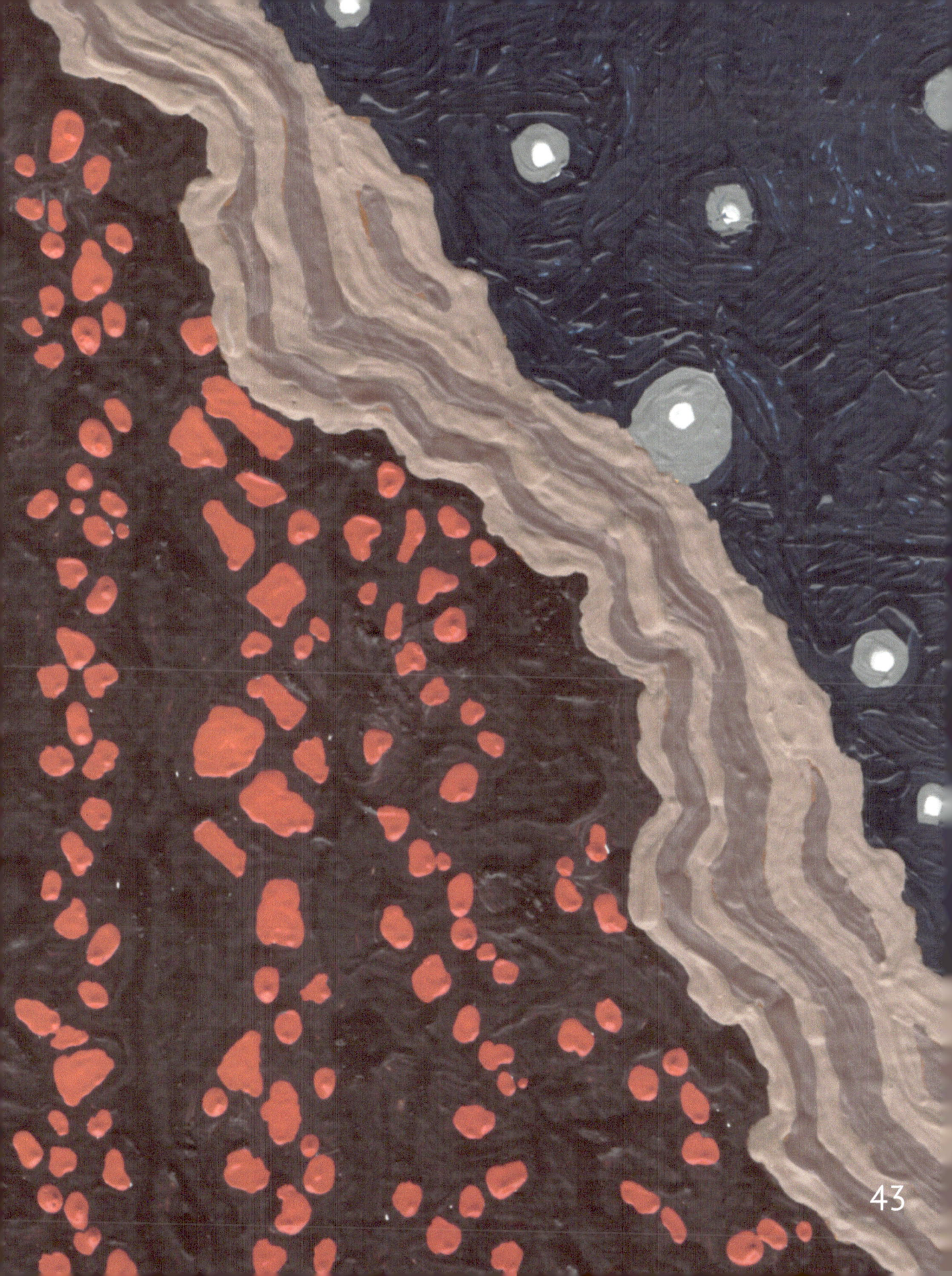

The eggs so magnetic;

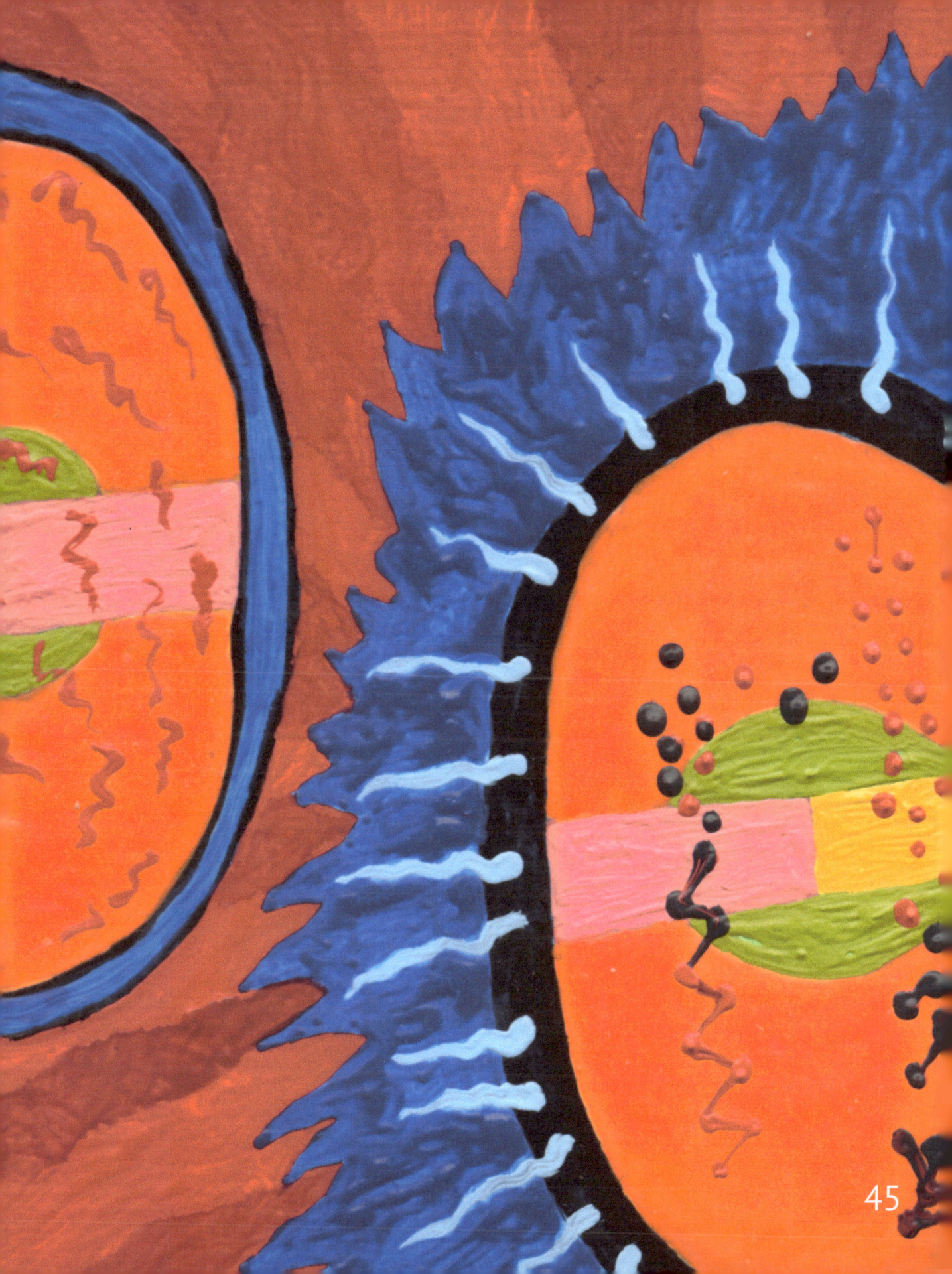

45

And the mitochondria so insatiable.

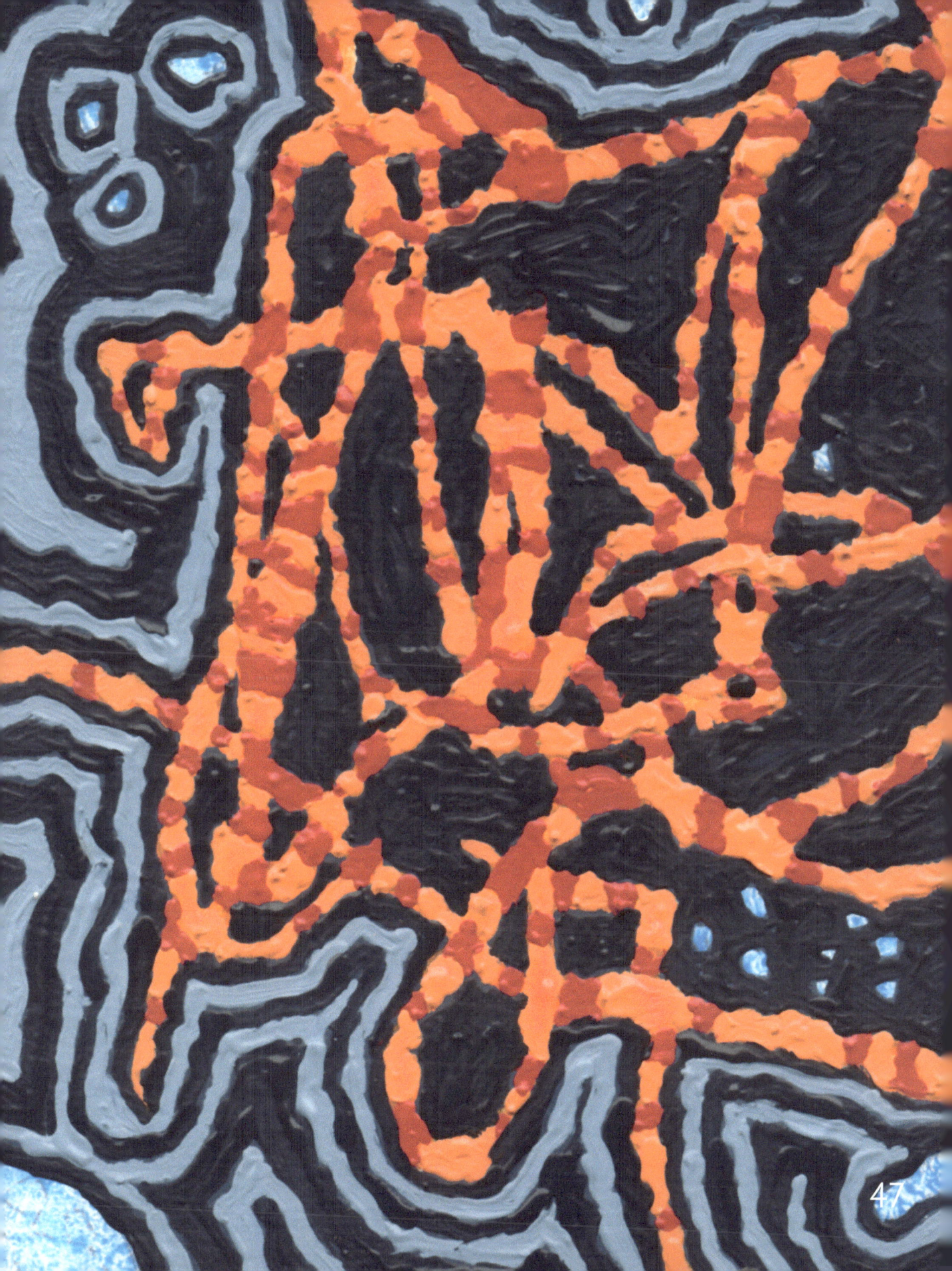

In the moment between
Being awake
And being asleep,
I saw the cosmos in the kaos

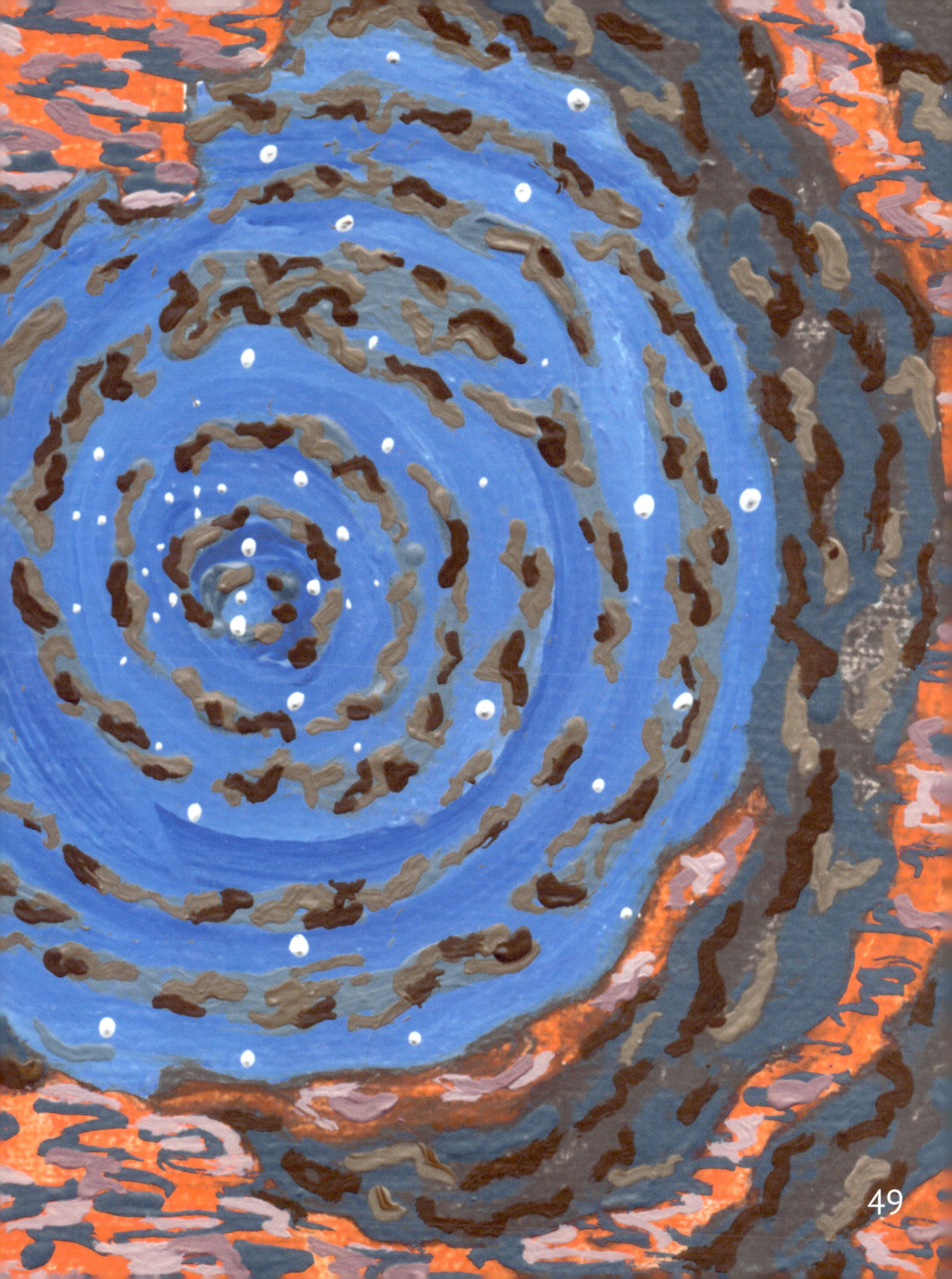

And the Kaos in the Cosmos.

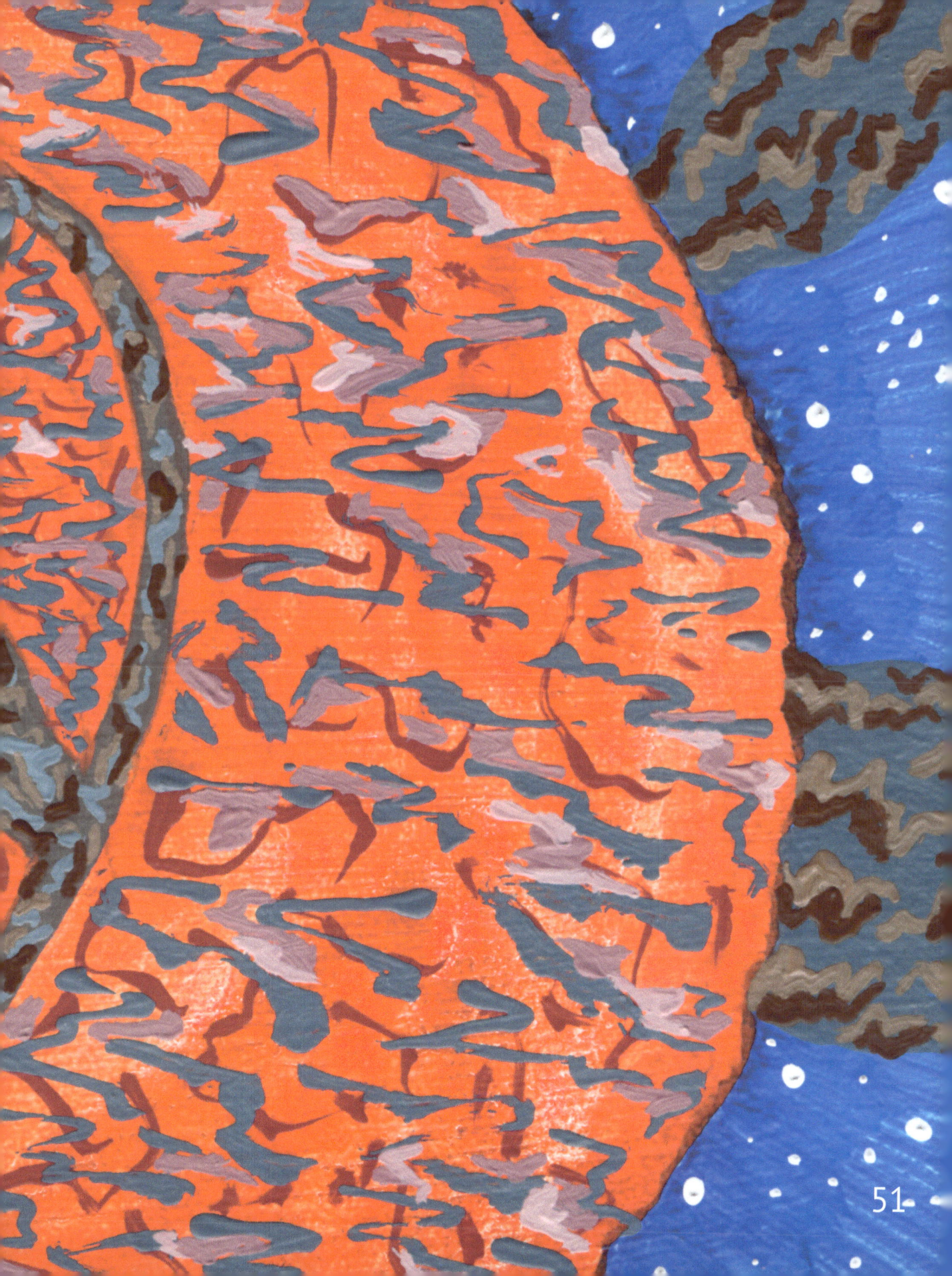

Looking away from the window
The inside and outside

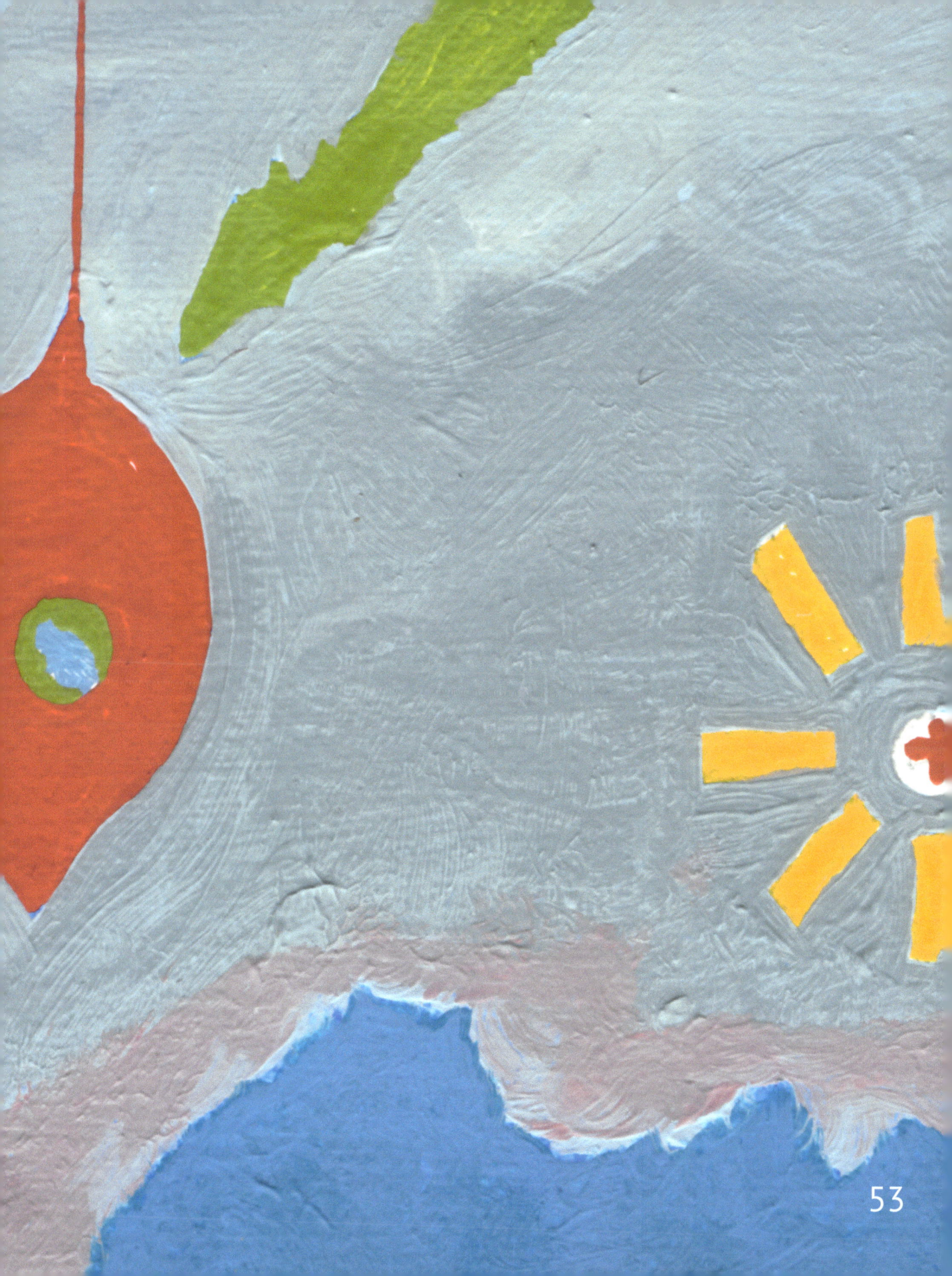

were reversed.

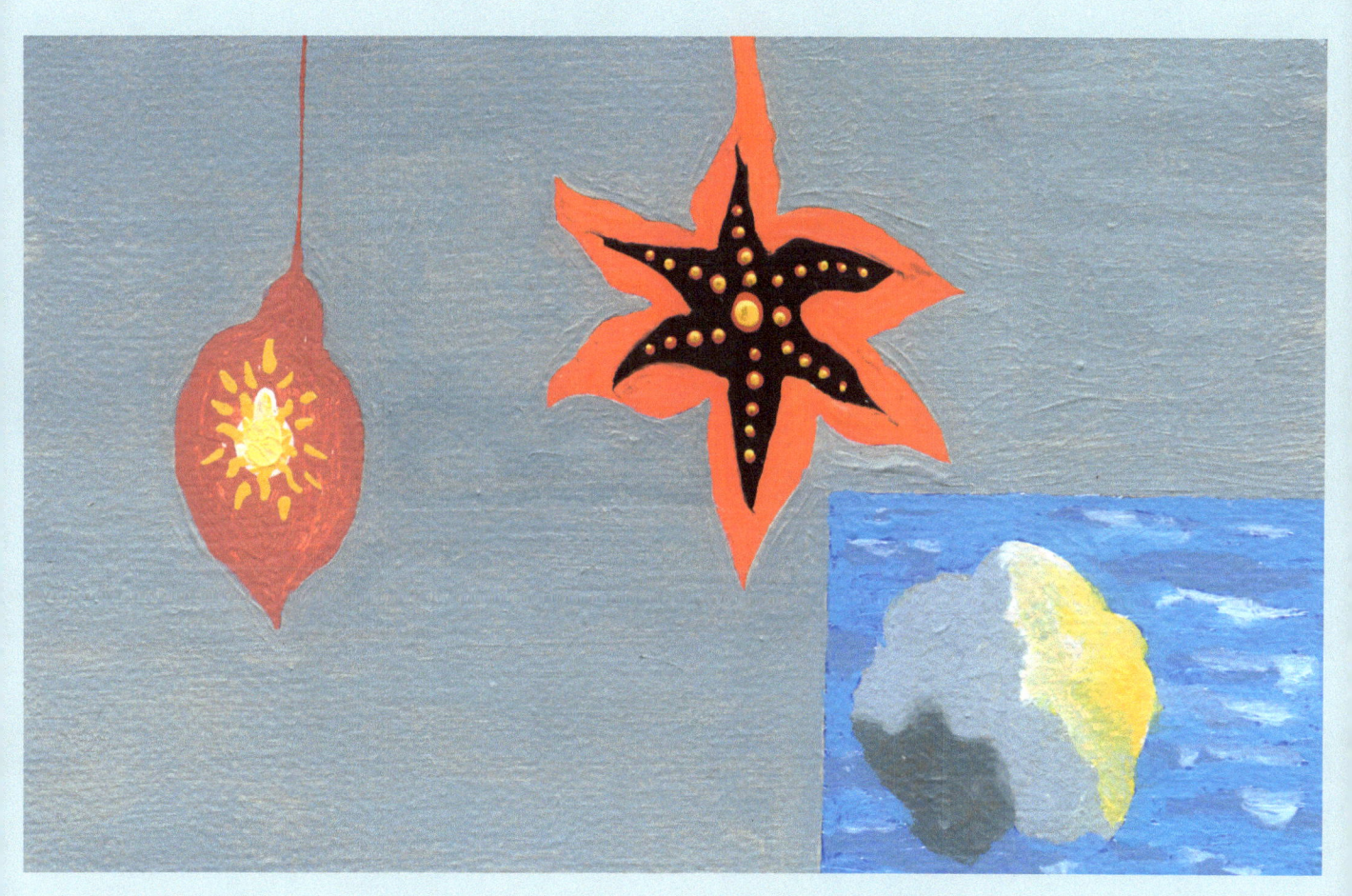

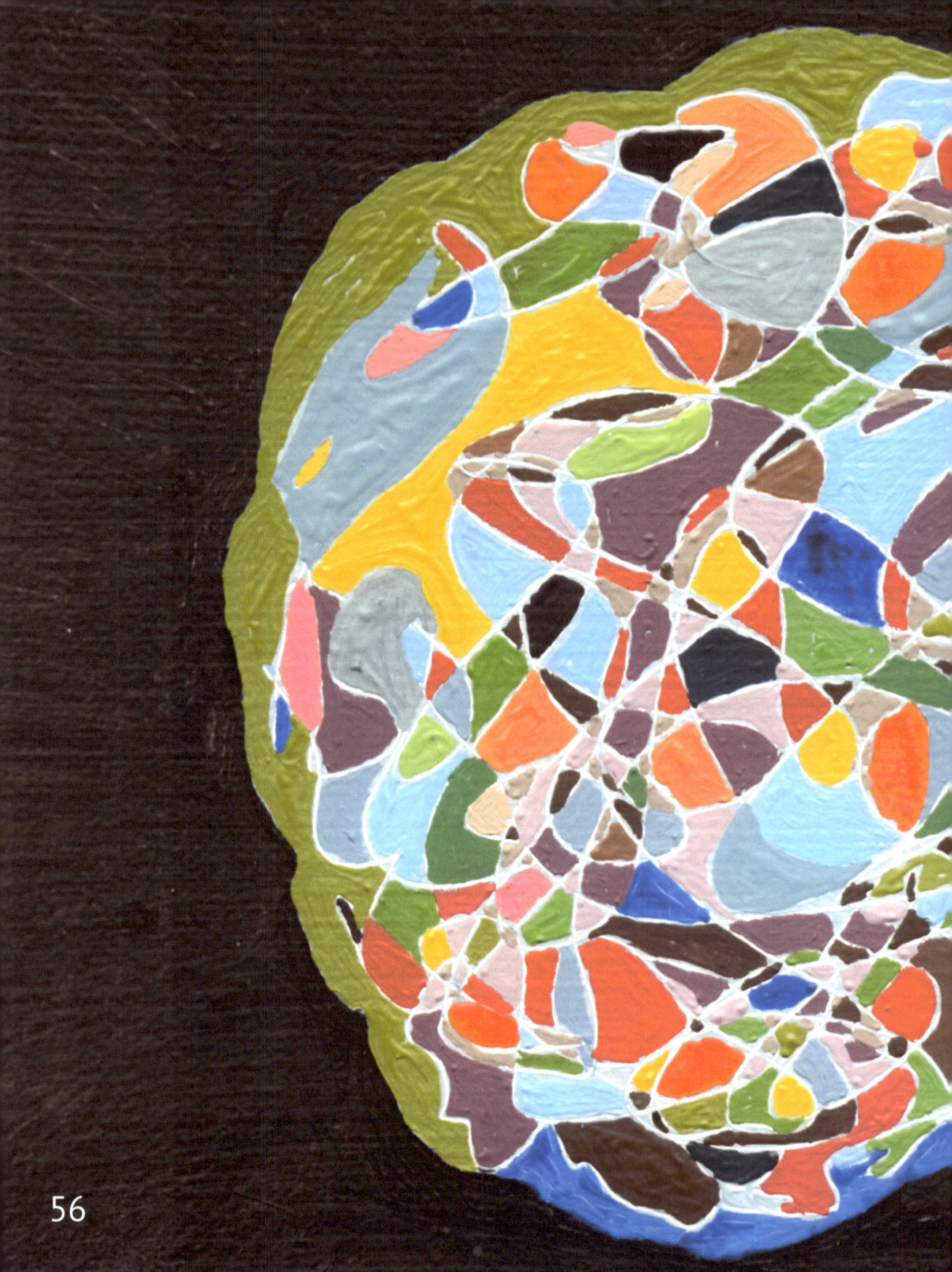

Contributions from Friends

1	Creativity Begins by *Lily Fürstenow*	*58*
2	Cosmos, Chaos and Improvisation by *Keith Harrison-Broninski*	60
3	Political Consciousness by *Jean Boulton*	64
4	Benign Catastrophe by *Robert Silman*	70

Creativity Begins
by
Lily Fürstenow

Text by Dr. Lily Fürstenow Ph.D. Co-curator of Yair Meshoulam's Show 'Cosmos & Chaos' in Gallery GH36 Berlin-Mitte.

Where chaos and cosmos meet, creativity begins. It's not a coincidence therefore that the recent exhibition by contemporary artist Yair Meshoulam is substantially influenced by these two concepts. The cosmic order versus the chaos of creation are an enormous source of artistic inspiration. The act of creation brings one closer to a sort of deity that engenders worlds on canvas. Yair Meshoulam's worlds are exuberant, vigorously painted with flamboyant colours. The abstractions bring the cosmic aspect to our worldly vision whereas the forms of flowers, houses and ornamental elements bear semblance to cosmic forms. The repetitive patterns on his textile collages make our gaze wander across surfaces in search of reiterating images.

Flowers drift reminiscent of constellations on the night skies, fairy-tale birdlike creatures soar across the picture surfaces as if flying in the mysterious firmaments above. Repetition and randomness in a swarm of lines remind one of handwritten graphic traces that dissolve in chaos. The traces spread all over the picture surfaces like pieces of land criss-crossed with the blue channels against the black backgrounds of the starry skies.

The accompanying poetic writing to Meshoulam's works acquires a particular significance as a means of communication but with no prescriptive message to tell, a mysterious code or an ornamental element recording the mark, bearing the presence of its maker as residue, as remains.

Anthropomorphic forms in the pictures of Yair Meshoulam analyse human bodily forms as mystic symbols. Some are similar to organic forms like flowers or animals e.g. the Wood Grain Series (see 'Textures of Consciousness' Volume 1 Tambar Press). Humans are considered to be the pinnacle of divine creation made according to the divine image of the gods. Constellations in the night skies are named after mythological heroes and stars are believed to be arranged to form human figures e.g. the signs of the Zodiac. What we believe to see in the sky during a starry night is the projection of ourselves into the space, our memory, our history. Yet, the higher cosmic orders are beyond our comprehension and knowledge. This ambivalence is obvious in Yair Meshoulam's pictures, it gives his work a certain spiritual dimension enhanced by the sombre colour palette of blacks, browns and yellows in this series of works.

Yair Meshoulam's use of flowers (as symbols of eternal bloom with ornamental inscriptions of some occult message) are difficult to decipher. Like stars blossoming up reminiscent of the ephemeral cosmic light that gradually fades away. The artist's colour palette is not intended to please conventional tastes that are used in traditional combinations of colours and forms, on the contrary the gaudy brightness of his cosmic landscapes, the loneliness and the fantastic creatures, flowers and houses question the notions of harmony and order, introducing a chaotic disturbing visual experience.

Cosmos, Chaos, and Improvisation
by
Keith Harrison-Broninski

Improvisation, whether with a musical instrument, a paintbrush or words, often seems magical to an audience. The greatest improvisers seem to be tapping into something unexplainable by normal rules – a well of inspiration and technique inaccessible to most people, no matter how long and hard they study and practice. What is actually happening when such performers improvise?

Let's start by defining improvisation as composition at sustained high speed. Sustained, since pauses may be taken but are constrained by the pace of the performance, for example to be measured in beats and fit into a meter - even sketching from life has a rhythm. High speed, since we would not consider as improvised a composition written one note per hour, a painting done one brush stroke per hour, or a poem spoken one word per hour – rather we consider improvisation as something that takes place faster than conscious thought, and that in some sense bypasses it.

This notion of taking place separately from consciousness opens up interesting perspectives on the nature of conscious thought. Given below is a famous improvised jazz break, Charlie Parker's astonishingly fast and intricate solo interlude after the band state the theme on the first recording of Dizzy Gillespie's tune "A Night in Tunisia".

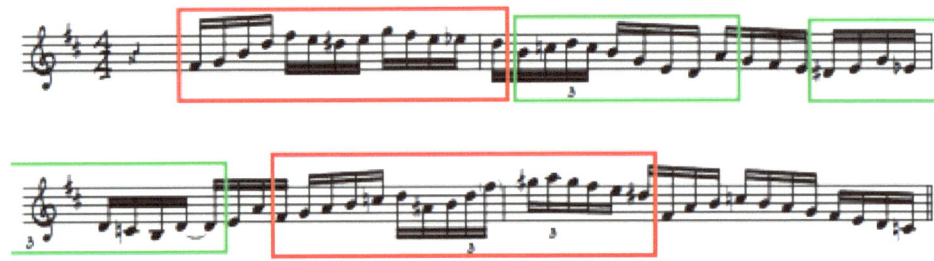

Even if you don't read music, compare the shapes made by the two sections in red - both start with the same two notes, then flow up, circle down and up, then down again. Similarly, compare the green sections – both start with a flurry up then down to the same note, and continue with an opposing flurry down then up. These are variants of what jazz musicians call licks, which they routinely practice in all keys, and which they come to know well enough to reproduce almost automatically.

Most improvising musicians, in musical genres such as bluegrass and rock as well as jazz, have a large repertoire of licks which they draw on when playing. However, a solo formed of licks reproduced without careful alteration is boring – jazz musicians dismiss such playing as running the changes, and musicians generally consider it to be pointless showing off. Charlie Parker's solo above is legendary not for its blinding speed, but rather for the way in which he combines, modifies, and elevates the licks into a stream of exquisite melody.

The judgement required to do this draws on deep musicality, part of which is the recognition of patterns at a higher level, guiding how to use licks to create real impact. Parker's solo strikes the listener as not just a series of linear patterns, but as something with higher-level form and intent. The structures that help provide such deeper meaning are often fractal.

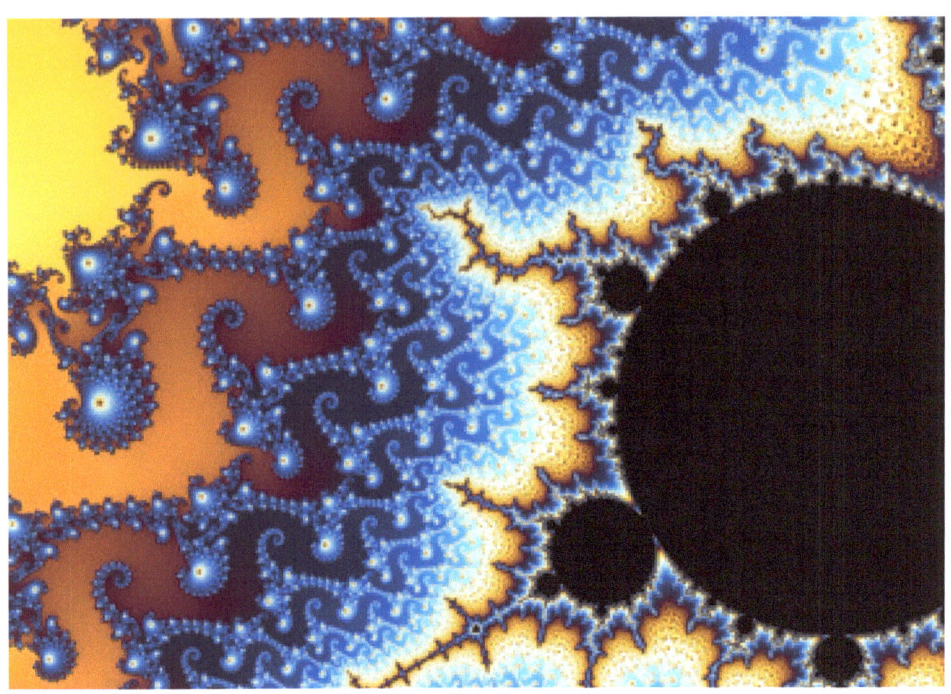

Shown above is part of the most famous fractal shape, the Mandelbrot set. It is fractal since you can look at it at any level and see similarity, from an overview of the whole down to examination of the smallest part. Fractality is fundamental to the mathematical theory of chaos, which has revealed order in apparent randomness throughout the natural world. From terrestrial structures such as snowflakes, trees, and coastlines to cosmic structures such as galaxies and spacetime itself, nature appears to follow fractal patterns – and when presented in music, art or words, we respond at a deep, instinctive level. Licks often contain self-similar patterns buried inside them, and musicians often combine licks in a way that mirrors these similarities at a higher level, as well as structuring their solos to contain even higher order symmetries. In art and poetry too, great works often possess strong self-similarity at multiple levels, which we respond to without necessarily being aware of so doing.

In principle, this sounds like a formula for generating great art - simply ensure that your solo, sketch, or poem is fractal and people will love it. In practice, it's much harder than it sounds, since improvisation unfolds in time - at sustained high speed, as per the definition above - and you can't go back to adjust anything. To improvise something fractal in front of a live audience is a real challenge.

When improvisers find themselves overcoming this challenge in performance, they often say they are in the zone. Being in the zone is very different to everyday thought processes. A common feature of current theories of consciousness is the understanding that many distinct things are going on simultaneously, each of which we are aware of to a greater or lesser degree. When you are in the zone, this awareness is replaced by a sense of being fully in the moment, and fully absorbed in a single creative process. Something about this singular focus helps make it possible to create self-similar structures on the fly – and being in an altered state conducive to fractal thinking also helps improvisers respond to others around them in real time.

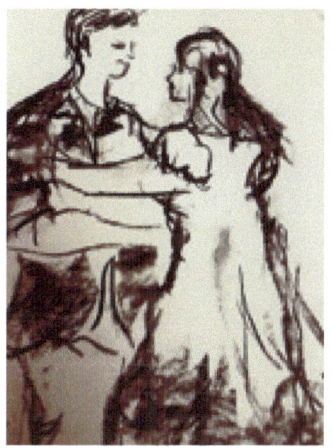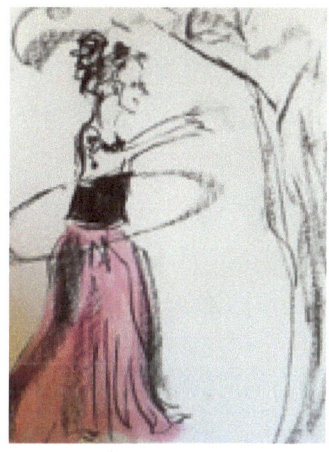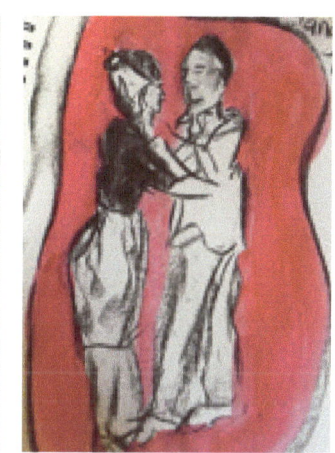

A feature of some musical improvisation is the immediacy in which band members can adjust to one another's playing, being able to stay in sync by switching tack with little apparent cue or advance warning. This may apply also to other art forms – for example, to drawing people dancing, as in the pictures above by festival sketch artist Ann Harrison-Broninski, or when a comedian whips an audience into hysteria. Signals are being transmitted and received not just with terrific speed but with a subtlety that may lie below conscious awareness. A jazz accompanist, for example, may not be aware of picking up such signals, and even listening back to a recording may not be able to detect what they responded to at the time.

People who can detect things about others that they should not be able to know are, sometimes thought of as psychic, and perhaps they too are responding to similar signals. If like improvisers, psychics are unable to trace back their intuitive responses to the source signals that generated them, then something cogent is crossing over a boundary, from an unknowable region into consciousness. This ability to formulate in clear language a concept that originates in the pre-conscious mind may offer a clue to the nature of consciousness itself – or rather, perhaps, to its multiple diverse natures.

Political consciousness
by
Jean Boulton

Consciousness - being conscious of ourselves in the world - is an important aspect of waking up, of noticing we are citizens in the world, participants in nature - as well as individuals and consumers. How we view ourselves, our sense of identity is, one can argue, the underpinning of our politics. For some, the issue of individualism, and individual rights is of paramount importance. Others seem born with a sense of responsibility for the world around them, for their role in creating the future. Where do we each sit in the terrain between 'liberté, egalité and fraternité' and how did we come to reside there? What is our personal political consciousness?

I was born in the north of England into a family whose roots were definitively working class, although my Father had done well in business and I and my brother went to fee-paying schools. In one sense, my parents and the extended family were not politically minded. They voted Conservative, in part I would suspect as they saw it as the way of the middle class. They believed in enterprise and graft as the path to betterment. Equally, my Father in particular was deeply and naturally community-minded. He helped people, he intervened, he stood up for those he felt needed his support. And he treated everyone the same. His strong sense of community and social justice (not words he would ever have used) rubbed off on me. I almost find it hard to imagine how you can not have a sense of responsibility.

Our political consciousness, then, seems at least to some extent to be constructed by, dependent upon, those early forces and influences that shaped us. And this political sense is visceral, before and beyond reason, deeply embedded in our tissue. I am reminded of the characters in Camus's 'The Plague', the story of the town cut off as plague had broken out. Some decided to make merry while they still could; others barricaded themselves in and hoped they would survive. And the doctor, who knew it would be hopeless, carried on helping people despite there being little point and knowing he would die in the attempt. These are all in effect political stances and Camus was exploring the varieties of human nature that underpins them.

I live in the town of Frome in Somerset. It has a fully independent town council. I am one of those seventeen town councillors. We campaigned as a group, emphasising that we were not for ideologies, or political stand offs between warring parties. We were for Frome. The strategy focuses on building prosperity, wellbeing and environmental resilience, and it is amazing what can be achieved at the lowest level of government through being creative with local resources and working with local people keen to make a difference. Frome has always had an independent vibe and it is interesting to consider where this comes from. What makes Frome so different? How can it be so vibrant, radical, energetic, full of art and passion and action when so many small towns around it are dying?

The early wealth of Frome, from the 16th century, was based on wool, and the town was bigger than Bath until 1650 and second only to Bath until 1831. Perhaps linked to its position as a key 'cloth town', Frome had a lively diverse nonconformist society. John Wesley preached there many times and reported that 'the people here seem more alive than most'. Belham (1973) believes that the reason for the emergence of this strong non-conformist culture was due to the sustained growth in prosperity which bred self-confidence. At a time in history when much of England was feudal, Frome had no Lord of the Manor so was not dominated by landowners and the aristocracy. It was the local clothier families who dominated society both economically and politically and many of these were non-conformist. Equally the cloth industry was essentially a cottage industry, with many weavers, dyers and carders working in their own homes; many were literate and independent-minded.

Frome was adversely affected by the rise of the industrial revolution in the nineteenth century and by the subsequent demise of manufacturing in the late twentieth century, not helped by its poor transport infrastructure and a geography that does not lend itself to large developments. However, a couple of wins for local campaigners paved the way for the future; one was a campaign to preserve a historic area of Frome called Trinity, which became a conservation area in 1973. This means that Frome has the highest number of listed buildings of any town in Somerset, and this has attracted, from the 1980s, a new professional class into Frome, looking for a cheaper alternative to Bath. Secondly, there was a campaign against the district council in 1983 who wanted to site a supermarket on the old cattle market site in the centre of town and so this area, also, has been preserved as an open space coupled to the Cheese and Grain, the old market hall, which is now a vibrant hub and community space.

Then came a shift in national politics. The Social Democratic Party (SDP) was founded in 1981 by four senior Labour moderates. For the 1983 and 1987 elections, the SDP formed an alliance with the Liberal Party. Nationally, the policy of the Lib-Dem Alliance was to involve local people in feeding into national policy and in grappling with what was needed locally. This created a new surge of interest in politics, both national and local, and really worked to bring politics to the grass roots. Sixty percent of the members of the SDP were new to politics. This was reflected in Frome by the fact that the Lib-Dem Alliance (and from 1988 the Liberal Democrats) won and held the majority of seats from 1987 until 2007, apart from 1995-99 when Labour had a majority. This inclusive bottom-up approach to politics, the core principle for the SDP founders, seemed to mirror the culture of independence in Frome from earlier times and perhaps points to where we are today.

So, my thesis, both for individuals and communities, is that, to some extent, political consciousness is shaped by history and gets embedded in our very fabric. Political consciousness is, indeed, often unconscious and our political beliefs can seem obvious to us, unassailable and 'true'. The political cultures of place and family are also shaped by the wider political ideologies in which societies become immersed. These are often based on theories of human nature and on attempts by political philosophers to make sense of their times (see Hardy, 2011). Machiavelli saw Man (not Woman) as in a perpetual fight for more, driven by desire. Hobbes and Burke agreed and felt that the State must counter such desires. Locke and Mill emphasised individualism and the need for freedom. Rousseau felt that people were born 'good' and were not essentially self-seeking. Socialists believed in equality as the central focus of political life. But which ideology appeals to us in often determined by our past experience and the beliefs with which we grew up. The careful nurturing, through advertising, of our role as consumer rather than citizen, encouraged to play our part by growing the economy and creating competition through our selfish choosing of what we want, is another more recent shaper of our political nature.

Is there a theoretical basis that would support this notion of the path-dependent emergence of our politics? This is a question dear to my heart. I write and teach about the 'new science' of complexity (Boulton et al, 2015). The core of these ideas is that the social and natural world has to be understood as in perpetual 'becoming'. What emerges is shaped by our history.

This is a very powerful idea that is, on the one hand, obvious, but also easy to forget. For example, the thinking behind the invasion of Iraq by the US in 2003 imagined that, if Saddam Hussein were removed, the Iraqi people would be ready to embrace the political and social ideas of the West (Schmidt and Williams, 2008). This was to ignore the rich social, political and religious history of Iraq and the region.

And yet this respect for history is not sufficient in itself. The established norms and patterns of behaviour that have emerged and become established are challenged and potentially destabilised, in the present, by the particularity of events, variations, decisions, shocks and so on that take place in particular places at particular times. This is in tune with the theory of evolution, where ecological patterns emerge and may stabilise over time, but the shape of the future depends on variation either within these ecologies or in the wider environment. The future is a dance between the power of current historically-shaped cultural patterns and the ways these destabilise and shift through variation, events, shifts and, in human systems, through the actions of particular people, through critical decisions and choices. There is an incommensurable tension between order and chaos, between fixedness and change, between sameness and difference, between the individual and the community.

Some politicians are very skilled at reading the deep frustrations embedded in society and seeing how to speak to these frustrations. Nietzsche said, of Napoleon III, that Napoleon 'was capable of ferreting out the hopes and dreams of the people with unerring instinct and fulfilling them in such a way that his boldest coups appear to be the will of the whole nation' (Safranski, 2002). In the West, these frustrations seem increasingly to be about economic inequality. For example, since the 1980s income inequality between the top 10% earners and bottom 10% in OECD countries has risen from 7 to 9.5 (Keeley, 2015). In the UK, top CEOs now earn 386 times the national living wage (Equality Trust, 2015). We, the ordinary people, construct narratives about what causes the unsatisfactory situations in which we find ourselves and, equally, construct narratives about what would solve them. One response is to feel that our reduced standard of living is caused by immigrants, coupled with giving money to institutions such as the EU or to international aid. 'We want to close the doors'. 'We don't want interference in our laws, and we relish our sense of nationhood'. The counter response is to envisage an increasingly open and connected world in which people can move freely and where equality will arise out of embracing a wider, inclusive community, seeing ourselves as free but connected. One can argue that both of these visions is emotionally-held and hard to argue against. Facts and information can seem to count for little. The politicians who speak to these strongly-felt envisaged futures and come up with simple solutions ('leave the EU and all that money can be spent on the health service' or 'build a wall to keep out the Mexicans') are the ones who often win, for good or ill.

So what do we do? Can we learn anything from this science of complexity? The answer itself is complex. On the one hand we need to take account of what cultural patterns underpin our societies and pay them attention, as in the example of the Iraq War. On the other hand, we need to spot where there are shifting trends, new attitudes emerging. Politicians may not pay sufficient attention to the strength of feeling regarding increasing inequality, to the flat lining of wages as costs continue to rise. Equally, they may underestimate how many young people have new attitudes towards diversity, towards travel, towards climate change. These emerging attitudes and the strength of feeling that underpins them can go unnoticed and it is the politicians who are alert to these changes who will be effective. If politicians only use evidence when it is 'certain' and stable and build on this to try to game the system through providing the voters with what they conclude voters want, their lack of integrity and conviction may show. As I write this, school children in the UK have been on strike for a day protesting at the lack of action about climate change.

The example of the schoolchildren raises an important point to be made about ethics and values. In a complex system, each action contributes towards the system and plays its part in shaping the future. And the future, whilst not random, is not certain either. To quote Aldous Huxley (1937):

'the end cannot justify the means for the simple and obvious reason that the means employed determine the nature of the ends produced.'

If we say one thing and do another, or if we skate the truth or manipulate others in order to bring about a particular outcome, then it is those actions and intentions that are added to the system. What we contribute is tangible, but we cannot ever guarantee we will achieve 'the end', the outcome for which we have worked and planned. This can create both a sense of humility (I cannot be sure I will achieve what I set out to do) and yet also a sense of purpose and agency (every action and intention counts). For those who value integrity, who want to create an equal and sustainable world, such as the schoolchildren protestors, any lack of integrity or lip service to such goals is likely to be sniffed out.

But there is another paradox here. Sometimes might and power win. There are innumerable examples, in commerce as well as in politics, where, once particular groups gain power and influence, they are hard to unseat. This locking in of patterns, without counter forces to challenge them, has contributed, one can argue, to economic inequality as global businesses dance around national boundaries in a world that is increasingly deregulated. And the lock-in of one-state politics is equally hard to budge. So how can ethically-informed, small, tentative steps counter these seemingly unstoppable forces?

One aspect of a response to this question focuses on the fact that even the most politically or economically entrenched systems can, and often do, in the end, collapse. For example, one explanation of the end of apartheid suggests that, after the fall of the Berlin Wall in 1989 and the collapse of the USSR, Russian diamonds flooded the market and the South African monopoly in their trade collapsed. Was it this loss of economic power that created the political writing on the wall and heralded a new era, and to what extent did that link with the fact that the National Party could no longer use communism as a justification for oppression?

I am reminded of Nelson Mandela. Mandela was imprisoned for eighteen of his twenty-seven years in a small cell on Robben Island. Apparently, the guards had to be changed regularly as they became so affected by who he was, by how he held himself, they were converted to his point of view. It seems he continued to be authentic, to act congruently with his beliefs, despite the fact that the 'end', the goal to which he had worked, must have seemed impossible, entirely lost from view. And yet he went on to become President of South Africa and guided the country out of apartheid. I have met South Africans from all backgrounds who are visibly moved when they speak of him; he is seen as a great man by very many people and he did, in the end, achieve his aims. Yet even so, it would be hard to argue that such a person and such a moment has wiped away the history of South Africa and its cultural patterns and divides. Shifting deep-seated patterns often has to happen one small ethical step at a time.

So, to conclude: political consciousness is strongly affected by history and context, both personal, local and societal. And yet this does not mean our political views and behaviours cannot change. We are the outcome of our past, and yet we are the co-creators of our collective future. The past shapes us but does not define us and the future is alive with possibility and promise.

References
Belham, P (1973) The Making of Frome: Frome Society for Local Study
Boulton, J et al (2015) Embracing Complexity: OUP
Hardy, J. (2011) A Wiser Politics: Earth Books
Huxley, A. (1937) Ends and Means: Chatto and Windus
Keeley, B. (2015) Income Inequality; the gap between rich and poor: OECD
Safranski, R. (2002) Nietzsche, a philosophical biography: Granta
Schmidt, B. and M. Williams (2008) "The Bush Doctrine and the Iraq War: Neoconservatives versus Realists", Security Studies
The Equality Trust (2015) Pay Tracker

Benign Catastrophe
by
Robert Silman

Chaos is a void, the formless matter that existed before the creation of the universe. The origin of the universe, the big bang, is the moment when the universe emerged from Chaos, when Chaos became Cosmos.

Then what?
The second law of thermodynamics tells us that entropy is what happens. Entropy is molecular disorder, or randomness, of a system; and the universe is such a system; and the entropy of the universe will steadily increase until thermal equilibrium is reached.

How does it end?
The Cosmos will end in an entropic doom where energy is uniformly dispersed, and no life exists. Entropy is the Cosmos infiltrated by Chaos; entropic doom is its destiny, and the Cosmos will return to Chaos.

Thus, the ontological cycle is Chaos… Big Bang… Cosmos… Entropy… Entropic Doom… Chaos.
I have previously argued that it is Knowledge which can (and does!) reverse entropy and the ontological cycle[1]. The force of entropy (Chaos) is opposed by another (maybe greater?) force of negentropy (Knowledge).

Since I am not a physicist, it's probably best if I move to an area where I have slightly greater understanding to address another issue where there is a similar opposition.

We know what the life cycle is. If we take the example of human life, we start as a fertilised egg, we grow as a foetus in the womb, we greet the outside world as a neonate, the baby becomes a child, somewhere between 9 and 14 we pass through puberty to adolescence, and we remain as reproductive adults until the menopause after which we age and die. We do not repeat our life cycle, our life cycle is repeated by our offspring.

We know what medical science is. If we take the human body, medical science considers it to be a homeostatic system where everything is designed to resist the forces that try to disturb it. If the temperature rises it sweats to cool itself. If it is deprived of water, the kidneys conserve fluid. Disease is the disruption of this stable state by a disorder (Chaos) in the system, like an out of control growth (cancer), or a mechanical failure in a part (heart attack). Medical science is directed to protecting homeostasis and opposing disorder. If our blood pressure goes up uncontrollably, medical science comes to the rescue and provides the ailing body a remedy (anti-hypertensives) to bring the system back under control. And so it should! Medical science is designed to keep things the same, to prevent the body from decaying into Chaos. Of course medical science is doomed to fail. Eventually our bodies must decay, and it is inevitable that eventually we do all die (the human version of entropic doom). However, medical science is there to reinforce homeostasis as a remedy against early death; and an 'early death' is just a synonym for 'premature Chaos'.

The question that needs answering is how the life cycle (which is all about change) is compatible with medical science (which is all about resisting change)? If homeostasis is the process which keeps everything the same, what is the process that allows things to change without the change being chaotic?

I have addressed this elsewhere[2,3]. In summary this is the thesis.

Just as Knowledge is the negentropy which opposes Chaos in the ontological cycle, so Catastrophe is the negentropy which permits ordered change to occur without Chaos in the life cycle.
This can be explained if we examine a life changing event. Puberty is an extraordinary moment in the human life cycle. Though it may take years for a pre-pubescent child to transform in to a

reproductive adolescent, the trigger which initiates the transformation, and without which it does not happen, is remarkably simple. It is a single event, the activation of the GnRH pulse generator in the hypothalamus.

GnRH is a hormone (Gonadotrophin releasing hormone) which is secreted in hourly bursts from one part of the brain (the hypothalamic pulse generator) to act on another part of the brain (the pituitary) to stimulate the secretion of other hormones (the gonadotrophins consisting of Luteinising hormone and Follicle Stimulating hormone) and these two pituitary hormones then stimulate the testes in the male to produce testosterone and the ovaries in the female to produce oestrogen and progesterone which are the end hormones resulting in puberty. Hence the transformation from child to adolescent, the phenomenon of puberty, can be reduced to a single event, the activation of the GnRH pulse generator.

The unanswered question is what turns it on? And even more important why is it turned on when it is turned on?

We can rule out maturation (whatever that means) as the answer because we know that the GnRH pulse generator is active in the foetus and turned off at birth. So there has to be some other explanation for why it happens when it happens.

The key to understanding the role of Catastrophe is to understand that homeostasis is never perfect. The homeostasis which keeps everything the same is bound to have within it a disequilibrium which is barely perceptible. My thesis is that Catastrophe (or in another context a tipping point) occurs when this disequilibrium reaches a point when it ceases to be unperceived; i.e. it reaches a moment when the disequilibrium has a consequence.

In the case of puberty, we centred our investigation on melatonin which is a hormone produced by the pineal gland, an organ situated in the centre of the brain. Melatonin is the hormone that regulates seasonal breeding in seasonal breeding animals and it does so because melatonin is secreted in the dark and the nights are longer in winter than in summer. So the change in the duration of the night time secretion of melatonin with the seasons activates or inactivates the GnRH pulse generator thereby providing the chemical signal for seasonal breeding.

Applying melatonin to human puberty is a different problem. Puberty is not seasonal, it is a once in a life time event. How could melatonin be a signal for a single life changing event? We investigated the secretion of melatonin in humans and discovered an astonishing fact, that melatonin secretion throughout life was constant[4].

Why astonishing? Because a constant secretion in a small body (child) would have a much higher circulating level than in a larger body (adult). In other words the disequilibrium created by a constant output on the one hand and an increasing body mass on the other passes unperceived until a Catastrophe (tipping point) is reached which triggers a whole new process which results in puberty. The following figure illustrates the model:

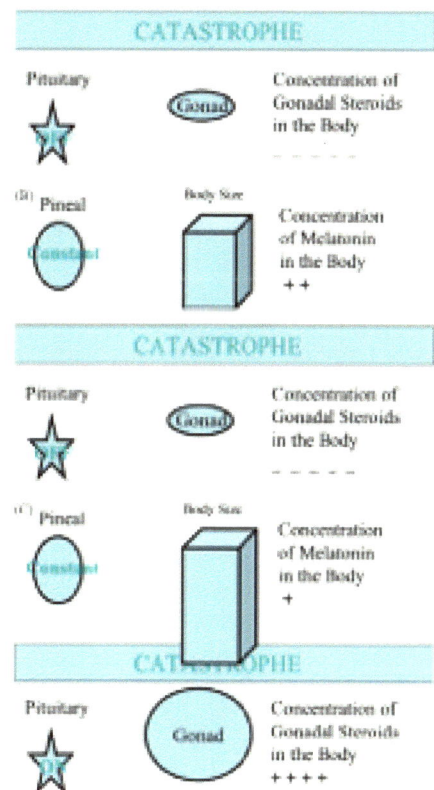

(A) An infant. (B) A pre-pubescent child. There is reduced body mass (small boxes). There is constant 24-hour output of melatonin from the pineal gland. The consequence is:
- high levels of circulating melatonin to
  - inhibit the hypothalamic GnRH pulse generator to
    - inhibit pituitary FSH/LH to
- inhibit the gonadal sex hormones.

(C) A post-pubescent adolescent. There is increased body mass (large box). There is constant 24-hour output of melatonin from the pineal gland. The consequence is
- low levels of circulating melatonin to
  - activate the hypothalamic GnRH pulse generator to
    - activate pituitary FSH/LH to
- activate the gonadal sex hormones.

To conclude:
For the Cosmos, change is malignant Chaos causing the disordered disruption of a stable state.
For a living being, change is benign Catastrophe facilitating the ordered sequence of a life cycle.

Notes

1. Silman (2015) 'Thoughts Without A Thinker' in Textures of Consciousness Y Meshoulam et al. ISBN 9781910133057 pp 90 – 97
2. Silman (1991) 'Melatonin and the human GnRH pulse generator' J Endo crinol 128, pp 7-11
3. Silman (2010) 'Catastrophe and homeostasis' Criminal Behaviour and Mental Health 20, pp 177-189
4. Young IM, Francis PL, Leone AM, Stovell P, Silman RE (1988) 'Constant pineal output and increasing body mass account for declining melatonin levels during human growth and sexual maturation' J Pineal Res 5, 71-85.

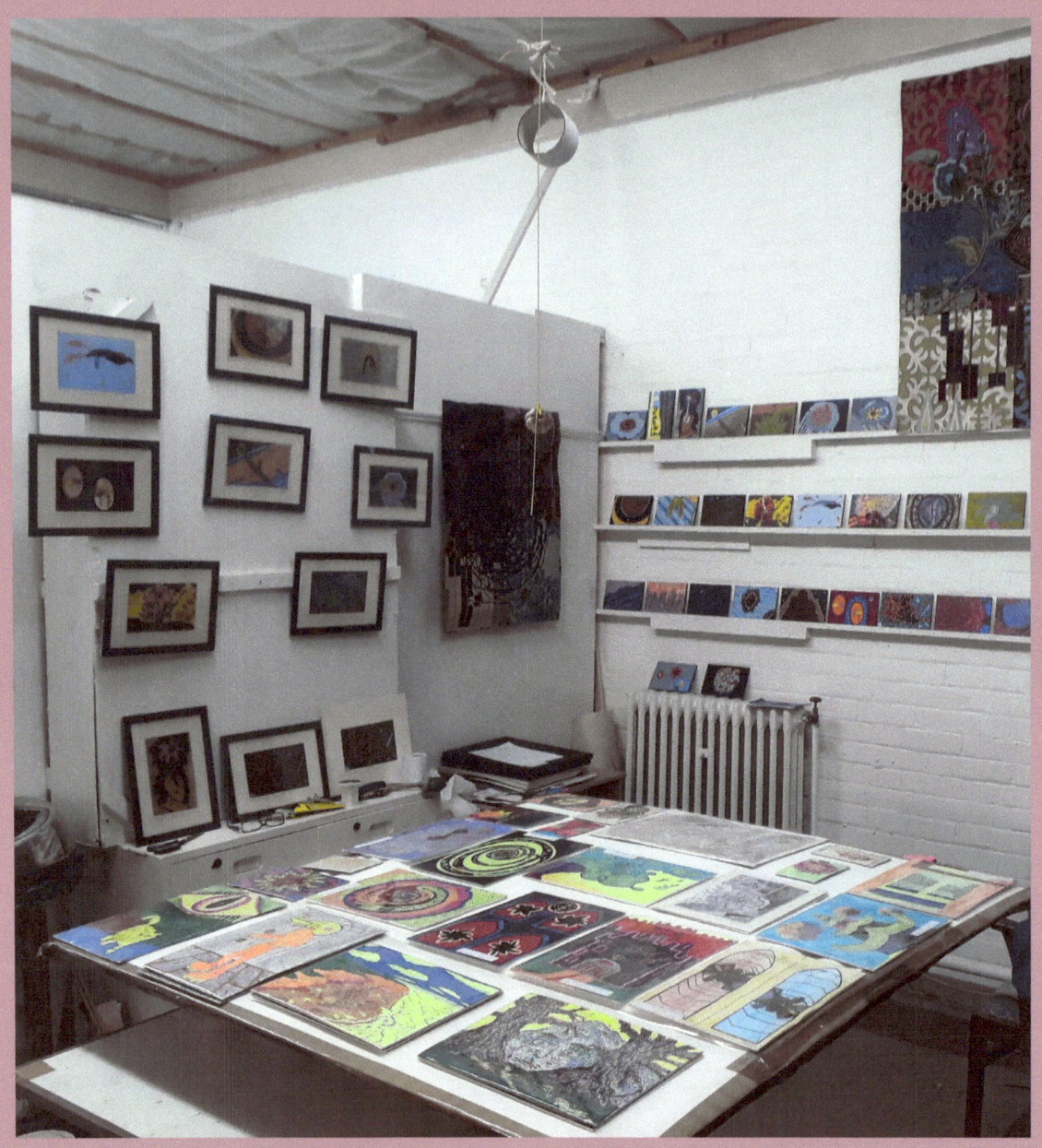
Yair Meshoulam's Studio: Acme Studio 10, Carlew House, 21 East Place, West Norwood London SE27 9JW

Index of Artworks

Index No.   Page No.

Index No.	Title	Page No.
1	'Cosmos'	1
2	'As I woke up and looked out of the window'	5
3	'Brain Flower'	7
4	'Solar Eclipse'	9
5	'Fixed Plants'	11
6	'Cloud of Cerebral Data	13
7	'The Reverse of Data is The Tower of Chaos'	15
8	'Photos from Saturn'	17
9	'Durdle Door'	19
10	'Moon Descending over Gaia'	21
11	'Lightening Struck the House of the Contained Body'	23
12	'Data Soul Bird'	25
13	'Volcano-god'	27
14	'My Heart remained beating but still'	29
15	'Fern of Action'	31
16	'Spiral of the Cosmos'	33
17	'Seas of Tranquillity'	35
18	'Undetected Pattern'	37
19	'The Moon and Earth seemed so purposeful'	39
20	'The Lilies so Intent'	41
21	'The Pyramids of Desire so Liquid'	42-43
22	'The Eggs so Magnetic'	45
23	'The Mitochondria so Insatiable'	47
24	'Kaos in the Cosmos'	49
25	'Cosmos in the Kaos'	51
26	'The Inside and Outside'	53
27	'Were Reversed'	55
28	'Chaos'	56

Artwork Index for 'Cosmos & Chaos'

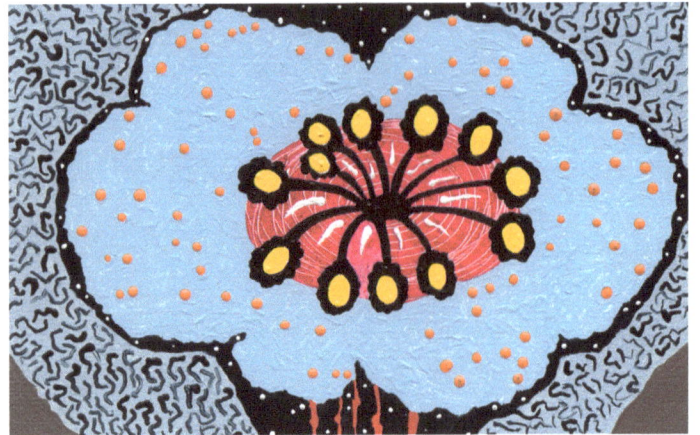

▲
1
1
'Cosmos' (2018)
Size: 21cm x 13cm
Medium: Oil on Board

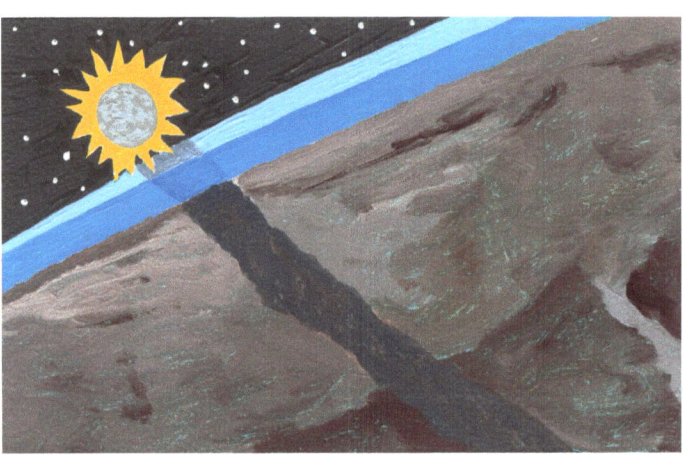

▲
2
5
'As I woke up and looked out of the window' (2018)
Size: 21cm x 13cm
Medium: Oil on Board

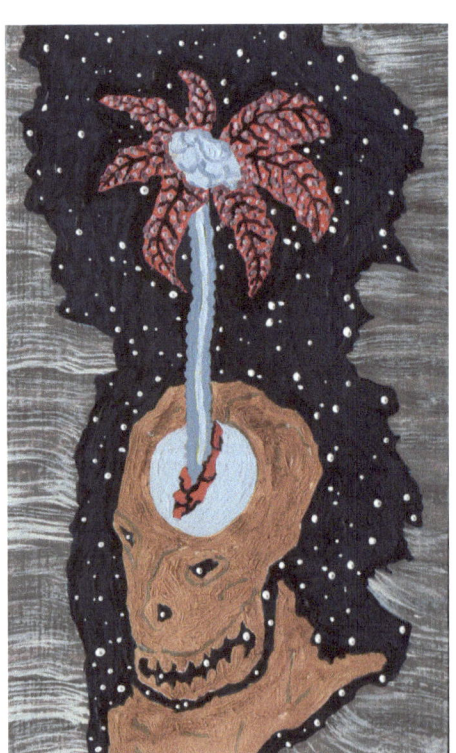

▲
3
7
'Brain Flower' (2018)
Size: 21cm x 13cm
Medium: Oil on Board

▲
4
9
'Solar Eclipse' (2018)
Size: 21cm x 13cm
Medium: Oil on Board

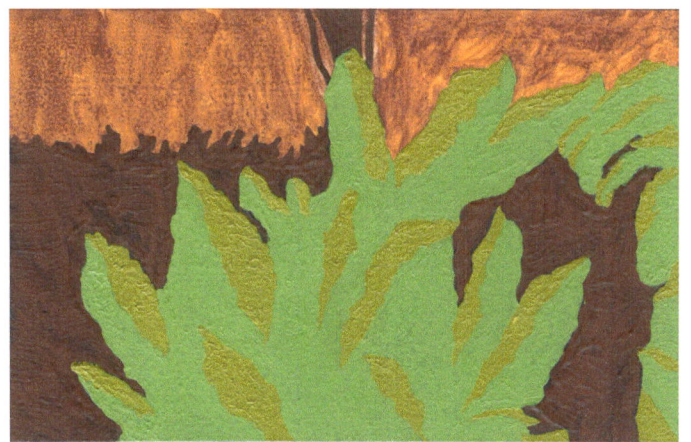

▲ **'Fixed Plants'** (2018)
5 Size: 21cm x 13cm
   Medium: Oil on Board
11

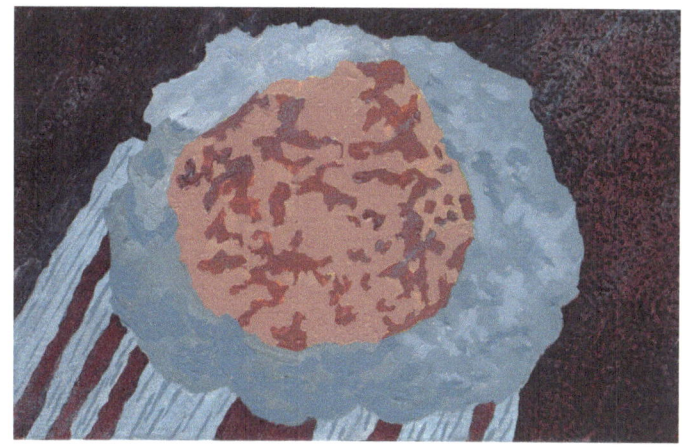

▲ **'Cloud of Cerebral Data'** (2018)
6 Size: 21cm x 13cm
   Medium: Oil on Board
13

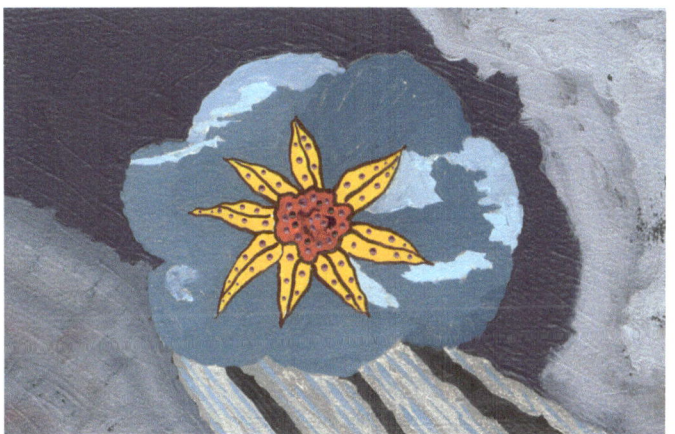

▲ **''The Reverse of Data is The Flower of Chaos'** (2018)
7 Size: 21cm x 13cm
   Medium: Oil on Board
15

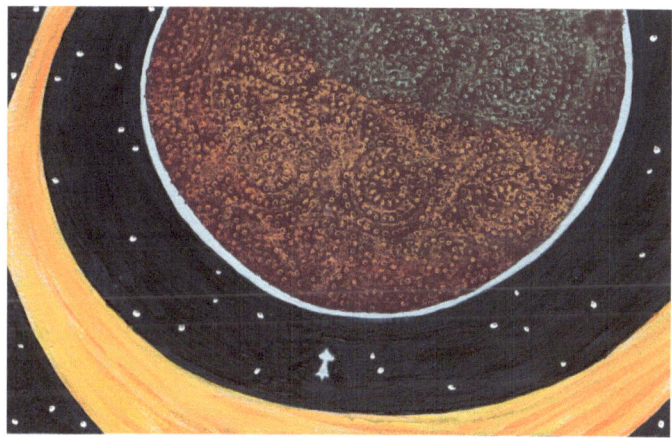

▲ **'Photos from Saturn'** (2018)
8 Size: 21cm x 13cm
   Medium: Oil on Board
17

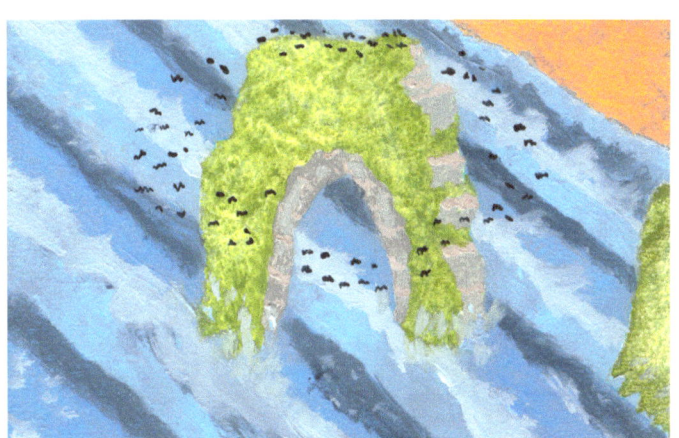

◄ **'Durdle Door'** (2018)
9 Size: 21cm x 13cm
   Medium: Oil on Board
19

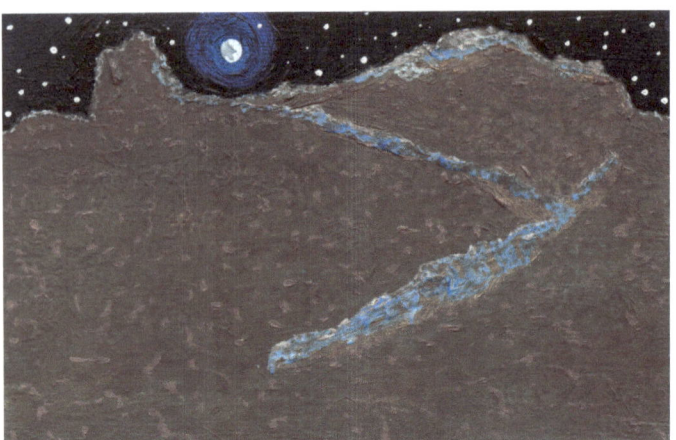

▲ **'Moon Descending over Gaia'** (2018)
10 Size: 21cm x 13cm
Medium: Oil on Board
21

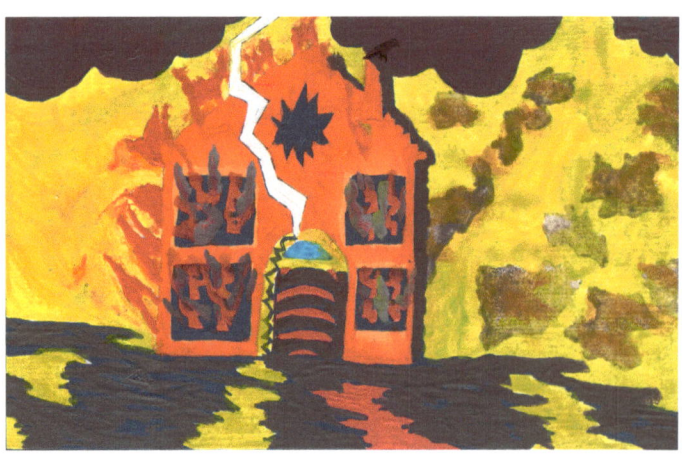

▲ **'Lightening Struck the House of the Contained Body'** (2018)
11 Size: 21cm x 13cm
Medium: Oil on Board
23

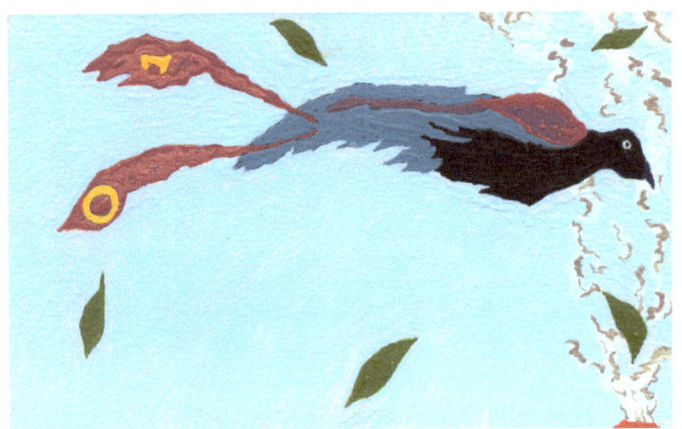

▲ **'Data Soul Bird'** (2018)
12 Size: 21cm x 13cm
Medium: Oil on Board
25

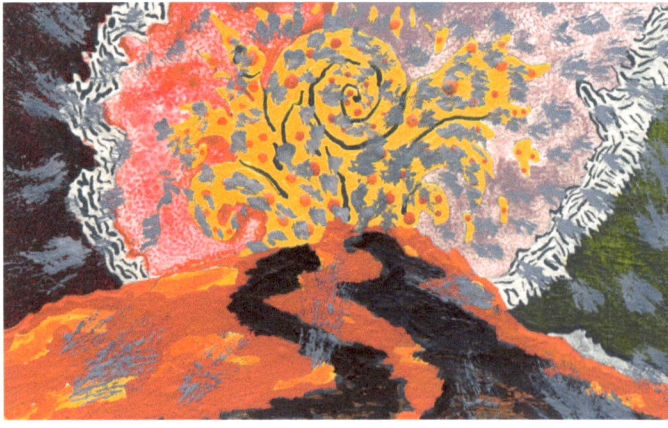

▲ **'Volcano-god'** (2018)
13 Size: 21cm x 13cm
Medium: Oil on Board
27

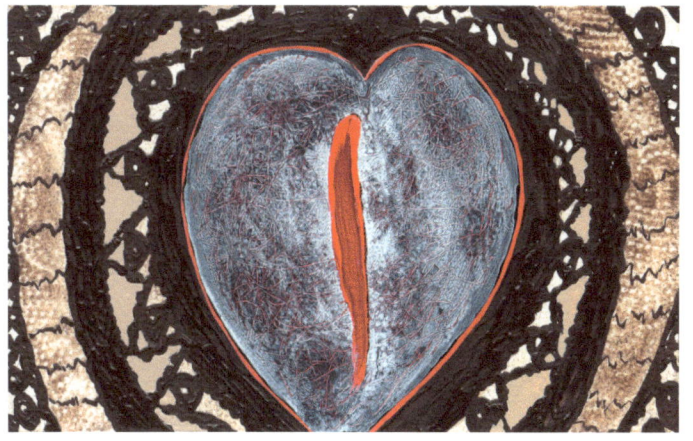

▲ **'My Heart remained beating but still'** (2018)
Size: 21cm x 13cm
Medium: Oil on Board

14
29

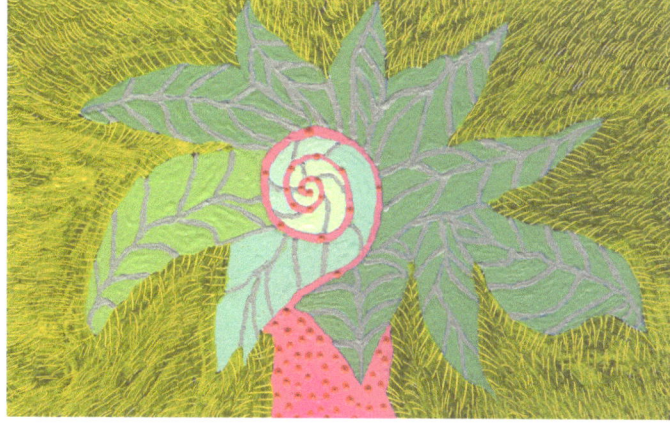

▲ **'Fern of Action'** (2018)
Size: 21cm x 13cm
Medium: Oil on Board

15
31

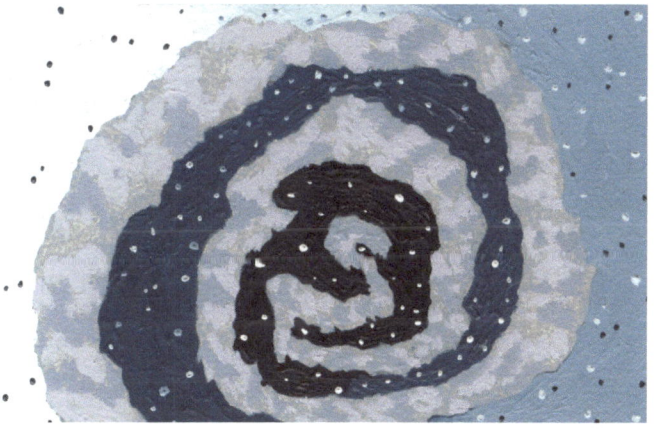

▲ **'Spiral of the Cosmos'** (2018)
Size: 21cm x 13cm
Medium: Oil on Board

16
33

▲ **'Seas of Tranquility'** (2018)
Size: 21cm x 13cm
Medium: Oil on Board

17
35

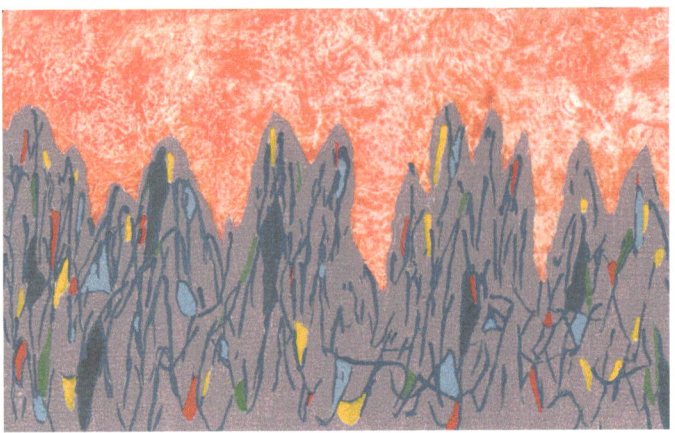

▲ **'Undetected Pattern'** (2018)
Size: 21cm x 13cm
Medium: Oil on Board

18
37

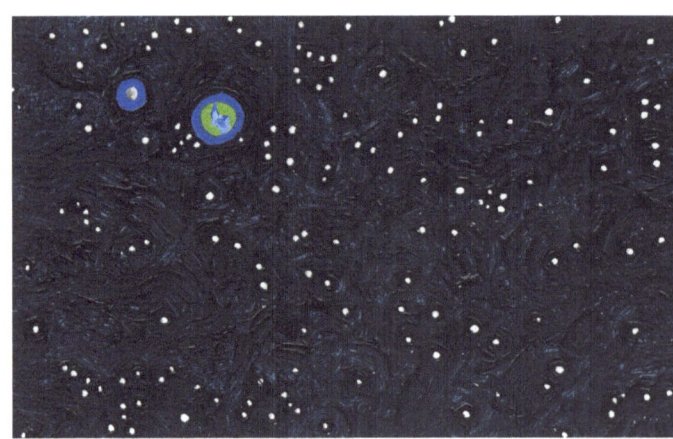

▲ **'The Moon and the Earth seemed so purposeful'** (2018)
Size: 21cm x 13cm
Medium: Oil on Board

19
39

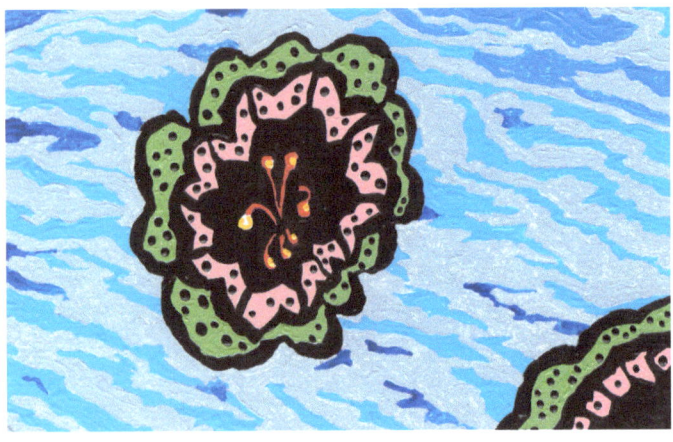

▲ **'The Lilies so Intent'** (2018)
Size: 21cm x 13cm
Medium: Oil on Board

20
41

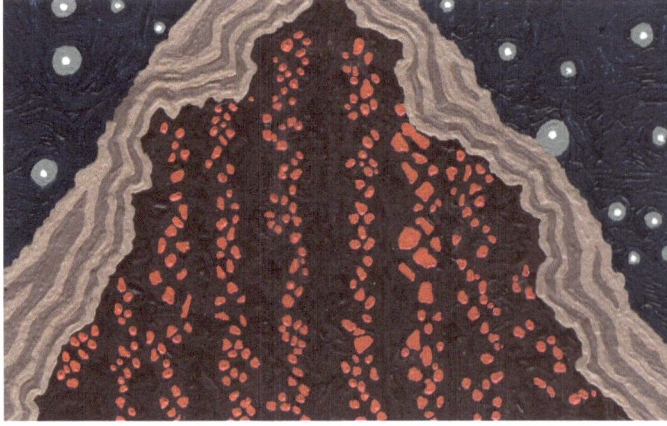

▲ **'The Pyramids of Desire so Liquid'** (2018)
Size: 21cm x 13cm
Medium: Oil on Board

21
42-
43

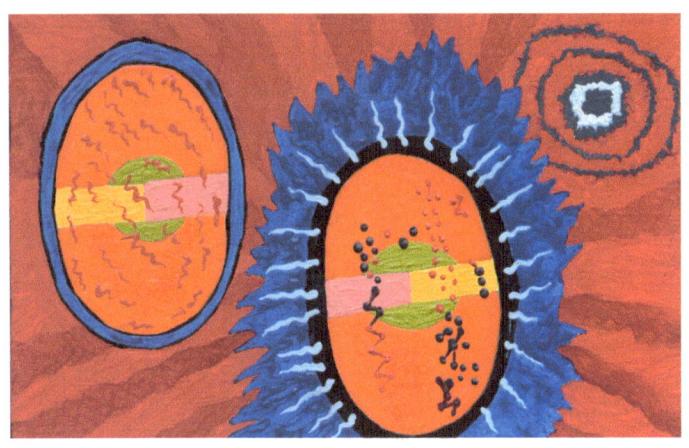

▲ **'The Eggs so Magnetic'** (2018)
22 Size: 21cm x 13cm
Medium: Oil on Board
45

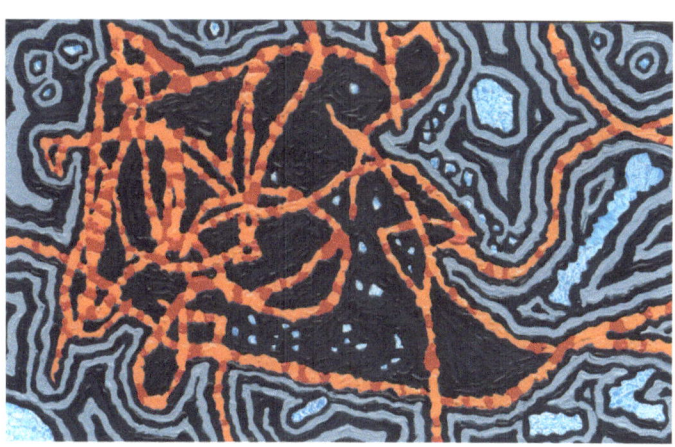

▲ **'The Mitochondria so Insatiable'** (2018)
23 Size: 21cm x 13cm
Medium: Oil on Board
47

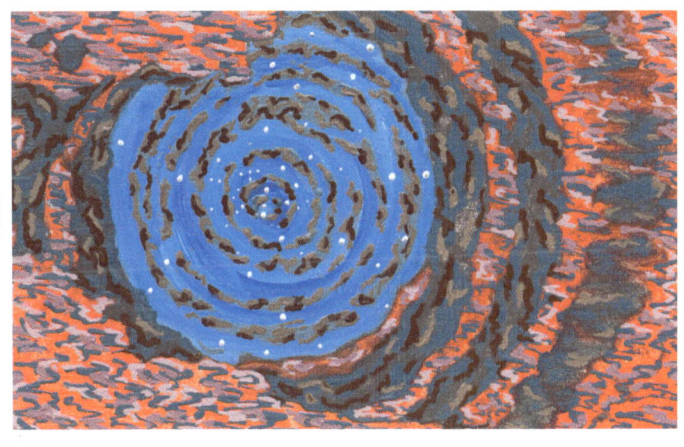

▲ **'Kaos in the Cosmos** (2018)
24 Size: 21cm x 13cm
Medium: Oil on Board
49

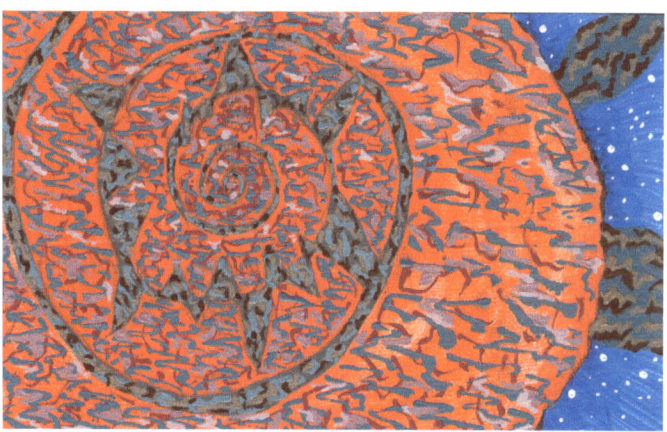

▲ **'Cosmos in the Chaos**(2018)
25 Size: 21cm x 13cm
Medium: Oil on Board
51

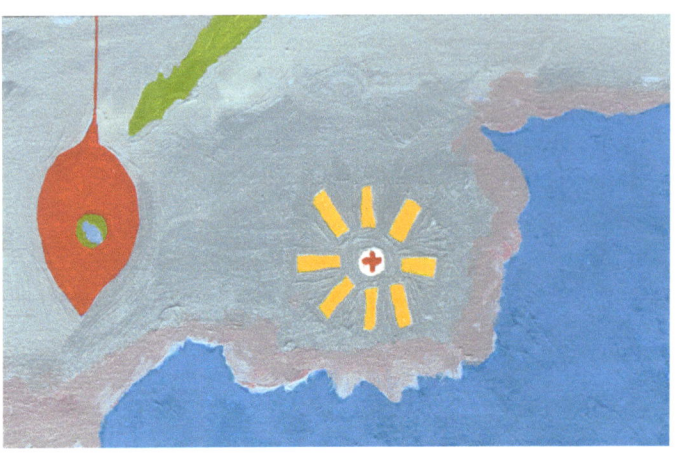

▲ **'The Inside and Outside'** (2018)
Size: 21cm x 13cm
Medium: Oil on Board

26

53

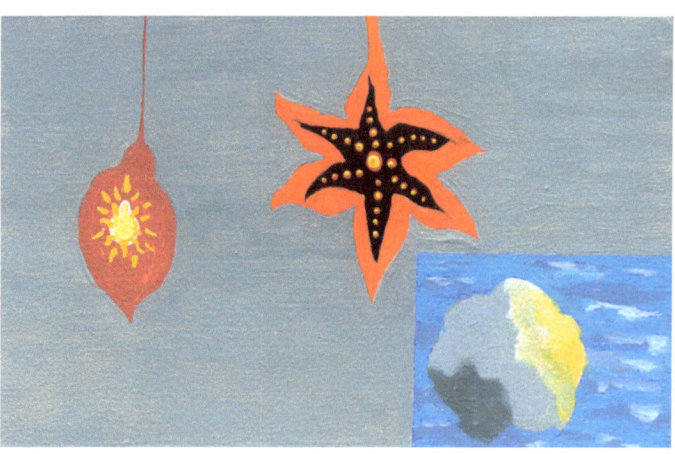

▲ **'Were Reversed'** (2018)
Size: 21cm x 13cm
Medium: Oil on Board

27

55

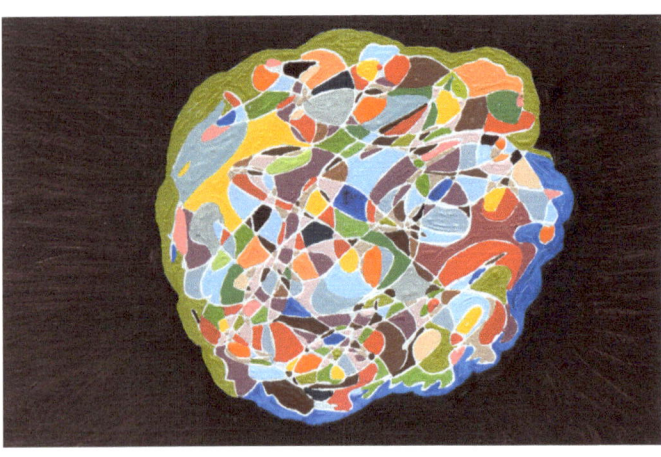

▲ **''Chaos'** (2018)
Size: 21cm x 13cm
Medium: Oil on Board

28

56

Biographies

1	*Yair Meshoulam*	86
2	*Lily Fürstenow*	90
3	*Keith Harrison-Broninski*	90
4	*Jean Boulton*	90
4	*Robert Silman*	90

Yair Meshoulam

Art School: Royal College of Art MA (Painting) 1986-88, Ruskin School of Drawing & Fine Art, BFA Oxford University Scholar 1982-5

Exhibitions:

2019 Solo Show & Book Launch 'Cosmos & Chaos -Textures of Consciousness Volume 2' Gallery GH36 36 GroBhamburgerStr. Mitte Berlin /Tambar Press. Co curated by Dr. Lily Furstenow e-merging artists.
Open Studios Acme Studios East Place West Norwood, London

2018 'Ink, Paper & Print' Fair, Winter Gardens, Margate.
Co-Curated Photographic Work Michael Sagel, Cafe Gallery MansteinStr., Berlin

2017 Group Show 'Curious SE27' Rosebery's Auction House West Norwood, London
Two Person Show 'Signs in Motion' with Martin Grover The Book & Record Bar, West Norwood, London.
Group Show 'Surface Explorers' at St Luke's Church, West Norwood, London all part of 'Curious SE27' Art Trail / Feast, West Norwood, London. Woolwich Contemporary Print Fair, Brocket Gallery Woolwich London. 'Talking Writing' The Book & Record Bar, West Norwood, London. Translation Work Videos LIS e.V. The Association – Help for People with Locked- in-Syndrome & Documentary about Michael Sagel English Versions Catalina Films Berlin.

2016 'Digital Wasteland' Video of 'House of Data' Shown at The Eiger Studios Gallery, Leeds curated by Sid Jim
https://www.youtube.com/watch?v=Jw97LzwwFxA
Open Studios Acme Studios East Place West Norwood, London

2015 Co-Curating 'Hand und Schrift / Hand and Written - Christine Kuhn 1953-2011' Galerie Luckstrasse, Berlin Group Show '40 x 40' GX Gallery Camberwell. Group Show 'A Letter in Mind' Neurology Appeal, Oxo Tower Gallery, Southbank, London. Solo Show with Book Launch 'Textures of Consciousness' (Tambar Press), The Record & Book Bar, West Norwood, London. Two person Show with Martin Grover 'Vinyl Cities & other stories', The Record & Book Bar, West Norwood, London. Solo Show at The Indigo Tree, Streatham, part of A23 Arts Festival. Group Show, Gallery 442, Streatham, part of A23 Arts Festival.

2014: Open Studio, Dulwich Open Studios, ACME Studios, Carlew House, West Norwood.

2013: Solo Show 'The Texture of Consciousness' Weekend Gallery, Charlottenburg, Berlin; Curating 'Christine Kühn 1953-2011 – Installations in Changing Times' Kesselhaus Museum, Lichtenberg, Berlin; Installation of photographic show 'Christine Kühn (1953-2013), Weekend Gallery, Charlottenburg, Berlin.
Open Studio, Dulwich Open Studios, ACME Studios, Carlew House, West Norwood; Art-Trail 'Collectables' 5th Avenue, Brixton Village Market, London

2012: Group Show, Portico Gallery, Knights Hill, West Norwood, London.
Two Person Show 'Arab Spring' Project The Weekend Gallery, Charlottenburg, Berlin.
'Curious' 'Spirit Bird Boxes', Art Trail, West Norwood Cemetery, London;
'Curious' Works on Paper, Portico Gallery, Knights Hill, West Norwood, London;
Co Curator 'Christine Kühn 1953-2011' Memorial Show at The Weekend Gallery, Charlottenburg, Berlin; Open Studio, ACME Studios, Carlew House, West Norwood, London;' Wallpapered

Furniture' West Norwood 'Feast' Festival & DoopoDoopo Forest Hill, London; Songwriting workshop Jerwood Art Space, Union St, London SE1 part of 'Now I gotta reason' events, with Steve Ounanlan & Pete Astor.

2011: Group Show, St Edmund Hall, Oxford University, Oxford; Dulwich Open Studios (ACME - Carlew House West Norwood);

2010: Late at Tate Britain, London. 'Shards of Utopia' Lecture/Performance/Music with Steve Ounanlan; Barbican in Ron Arad Show Lecture/Performance/Music with Steve Ounanian; Stoke Newington International Airport, London. Lecture/Performance/Music with Steve Ounanian; LondoNewcastle Project Space, Redchurch St E2 'Subverting Belief' Lecture/Performance/Music with Steve Ounanian, curated Cecilia Wee/ Neville Brody; The Incredible Trip to The Holy Mountain, Arts Admin Toynbee Whitechapel, London. Lecture/Performance/Music with Steve Ounanain: Group Show Elm Green School, West Norwood, London.

2009: Group Show Lambeth Open London; Video Web project Bureau de Change' Bank of Hope http://www.stevenlevon.com/?cat=16

2008: Two Person Show 'Wall Street', Bureau de Change, Shunt, London Bridge, London; Urban Arts, Brixton, London.

2007: Open Studio ASC 246 Stockwell Road Brixton London.

2006: Group Show 'Technology of Enchantment' Gallery CVA @ Menier Chocolate Factory London; 'Around the Houses Two' Brixton, London.

2005: Group Show 198 Gallery Brixton London; Group Show IJAYA (International Jewish Artists of the Year Awards) Ben Uri Gallery @ Tram Studios Camden Town, London; Open Studio ASC 246 Stockwell Road Brixton London.

2004: Open Studio ASC 246 Stockwell Road, Brixton, London; Group Show, 198 Gallery, Brixton, London.

2003: Selected Group 'Director's Choice' - Work to be purchased by the Ben Uri Collection, London.

2003: Selected Group Show, Limmud, Conference, Bromley College, Kent.

2002: Selected Group Show, 291 Gallery Hackney, London.

2001: Selected Group Show, Ben Uri, Jewish Artist of the Year, Angel, London; Selected Group Show, 'Secret', RCA, London Bowieart.com/Time Out.

2000: Selected Group Show, 'Contemporary Ceremonial Art', Succah, Jewish Museum, Camden Town, London.

1999: Selected Group Show, 'Jewish Magic and Mysticism', Jewish Museum, Camden Town, London. House Show, Brixton, London.

1998:   Solo Show 'Androids, Robots and Golems' Trevelyan College, Durham University, Durham;
        Solo Show Works on Paper 1988-1998 Ozten Zeki Gallery, Brompton Cross, London; Group Show
        Ozten Zeki Gallery, Brompton Cross, London; Open Studio Show, Parade Mews Studios,
        Tulse Hill, London.
1997:   Solo Show 'Robots', Ozten Zeki Gallery, Brompton Cross, London; Group Show, Ozten Zeki Gallery,
        Brompton Cross, London; Group Show, Connoisseur Gallery, London.
1996:   Two Person Show, Städtische Gallerie Haus Seel, Public Art Gallery, Siegen, Germany;
        Whitechapel Open Studios, ACME Childers Street Open, New Cross, London;   Group Show, Fitch's
        Ark, Little Venice, London; Group Show, 'Beyond England' - Internationally Exhibited Art
        RCA Graduates, Hockney Gallery, London; Group Show, Art Connoisseur Gallery,
        Marylebone, London.
1995:   Two Person Show, Curated by Julia Weiner, Boston Consultancy, Mayfair, London;
        Single Stall, Alternative Art Market, Alternative Arts, Spitalfields Market, London; Ben Uri Open,
        Ben Uri Gallery, Dean Street, Soho, London; Two Person Show, 'As Above, So Below',
        Ben Uri Gallery, Soho, London; Group Show, House of William Blake, South Molton St.,
        London; Group Show, Atrium Gallery, Whiteley's, Queensway, London.
1994:   Berlin/London Exchange Group Show, British Council, Bahnhof Westend, Berlin;
        Ben Uri Open, Dean Street, Soho, London; Group Show, Atrium Gallery, London.
1993:   Whitechapel Open Studios, 'Diagrams of Splendour', Childers Street, London;
        Ben Uri Open, Ben Uri Gallery, Dean Street, Soho, London; Group Show, Slaughterhouse Gallery,
        Smithfields, London; Group Show, Smith's Gallery, Covent Garden, London;
        Group Show, Hyde Park Gallery, London; Group Show, The Gallery, Mayfair, London.
1992:   Selected for Whitechapel Open, Whitechapel Gallery, London;
        Group Show, London Connection', Kassel (during Documenta), Germany;
        Group Show, 'Bloom', European Outposts, Spitalfields, London;
        Two Person Show, Gallery 47, Bloomsbury, London;
        Whitechapel Open Studios, Tower Bridge Studios, London;
1991:   Two Person Show, Ozten Zeki Gallery, Brompton Cross, London;
        Three Person Show, Gallery Dagmar, Dulwich, London.
        Group Show, 'Utopias', Gallery Dagmar, Dulwich, London Gallery, London
        Group Show 'Pictures on the Railings', Dagmar/ Dulwich Picture Gallery, London;
        Group Show 'East Meets West', Smith's Gallery, Covent Garden, London.
1990:   Portobello Open, Tabernacle Gallery, Portobello Road, London.
1989:   Selected for Whitechapel Open, Whitechapel Gallery, London;
        Three Person Show, Gallery Dagmar, Dulwich, London;
1988:   Degree Show, Painting Department, Royal College of Art, London.

Awards:
1982-1985 Scholarship, St. Edmund Hall/Ruskin, Oxford University.
Collections: Public - Sure Start, Lambeth Education London; Oxfordshire Health Authority, John Radcliffe Hospital; St. Edmund Hall, Oxford University; Private - Simmonds; Dr Brian Whitton, Micro Biologist (Durham University) & Art Historian, Author of British Surrealist 'Tunnard'; Chandris.

Teaching:

Winchester School of Art, Foundation Course, Visiting Lecturer. Winchester School of Art, Art History Course; Visiting Lecturer. Summer School Robin Child Norwich, Wiltshire, Cambridge; Workshops Rosendale Primary School, South London Artweek.

Publications:

2017 'Talking Writing' Collection Blundell/Seshadri/Potts/McGlasshan/Haney BRB WN
 'Ode to the South Circular' Dymo intervention.
2015 'Textures of Consciousness by Yair Meshoulam & Friends' Tambar Press ISBN 978-1-910133-05-7
2013: Kaltblut Magazine. September Issue. Review of "Texture of Consciousness'
 Show Weekend Gallery Berlin.
2000: Succah Panels – Jewish Ceremonial Art, Jewish Museum ISBN 953312910
1999: Contributor, 'Fold, Newspaper of the Unconscious ISBN 1466-4089
1998: Catalogue Solo Durham Show, 'Androids, Robots & Golems',
 Meshoulam/Reid/Weiner ISBN 0953312909.1997: Jewish Chronicle,
 'Making their mark, up and coming Jewish Artists', Julia Weiner. 1996:
 Siegen Zietung Newspaper; Westfalen Rundschau; Westfalen Post;
 Reviews of Seigen Show, Germany.1995: Catalogue Ben Uri Gallery 'As Above, so Below' –
 Images inspired by the Kabbalah GLR Radio Interview; Jewish London item on
 Kabbalah, discussion & review of Ben Uri Show; Ham & High Newspaper Review of
 Ben Uri Show, 'Magic and Morality', LindaTalbot.1994: Catalogue British Council Show in Berlin;
 'Arrival'. Der Tagespiegel, Berlin Newspaper Review, Katrin Bettina Muller.1993: Catalogue Childers
 Street Show, 'Diagrams of Splendour, Paintings from the Zohar' Kabbalah;
1992: Catalogue Gallery 47 Show, 'Little Flowers of St Francis'; Catalogue Ozten Zeki Gallery,
 'Biblical Paintings' ;Guardian Newspaper Whitechapel Open Review, Whitechapel Gallery,
 'Under Eastern Eyes' Tim Hilton; New Statesman. Whitechapel Open Studios Review, David Langsam.

Video links:

2017 'The Never Ending Traumatic Cycle of War' **https://www.youtube.com/watch?v=QMrjN0qQ6tg**
 'Signs in Motion' **https://www.youtube.com/watch?v=lCYSWhAeYQ0**
 'Surface Explorers' **https://www.youtube.com/watch?v=lfDEzE4BIcU**
2016 'House of Data' **https://www.youtube.com/watch?v=Jw97LzwwFxA**
2014: 'Yair : I am a painter' Directed by Jose Silver **https://www.youtube.com/watch?v=q7D5O8CEunY**
 http://vimeo.com/94775773

Websites:

www.yairmeshoulam.com www.textureofconsciousness.com www.wallpaperhangers.org.uk
Instagram: https://www.instagram.com/yairmeshoulam/
Facebook: https://www.facebook.com/WeekendGalleryLondonBerlin/

Lily Fürstenow

An art critic and curator for contemporary arts working in Berlin and internationally. After studying languages and cultural studies at the State Universities in Tbilisi, Georgia and at the State University of Vienna she was awarded DAAD Scholarship for research at the Humboldt-University Berlin, where she obtained her PhD Degree. Dr Fürstenow is the founder of the ARE/Artistic Research Encounters, which is the online platform offering virtual exhibitions for artists across the world and supporting creative exchange between art critics, artists and collectors. In her curatorial projects she focusses on museum collections and possibilities of artistic interventions, on the role of art in contemporary societies and on the challenges of arts and science. She has organised and co-curated exhibitions in various museums and institutions in Europe, including Museum Reinickendorf and Museum Domäne Dahlem in Berlin, Teater am Olgaeck in Stuttgart, Palazzo Zenobio in Venice and others.
ARE: http://artisticresearchencounters.blogspot.com/2019/04/georgian-artists-exhibition-palazzo.html

Keith Harrison-Broninski

His book "Human Interactions" is the only theory of organisational collaboration based on formal principles. His social enterprises aim to improve society via collaboration theory, the latest being stakeitback, tech to unlock new sources of investment into communities. He plays jazz on piano, traditional folk on English concertina, and composes in multiple genres.
Human Interactions: The Heart And Soul Of Business Process Management: How People Really Work And How They Can Be Helped To Work Better (2005) Meghan-Kiffer Press ISBN-13: 978-0929652443
http://keith.harrison-broninski.info/

Jean Boulton

A visiting Senior Research Fellow with the Department of Social and Policy Sciences at the University of Bath. She teaches, writes, consults and researches in complexity theory and its application to the social and natural world and is lead author of "Embracing Complexity"(OUP, 2015). Her work centres on how to live and work in a world that is increasingly volatile, interconnected and uncertain. As part of this she has been involved in local politics with a group of Independents and is interested in how localism plays its role in a global world.
Embracing Complexity: Strategic Perspectives for an Age of Turbulence (2015) Oxford University Press ISBN-13: 978-0199565269

Robert Silman

Obtained a degree in Philosophy at the Sorbonne where he was a student of Jean-Francois Lyotard, returned to London to train as a medical doctor. From 1980 to 2000 Senior Lecturer and Honorary Consultant at St Bartholomew's and the Royal London Hospital Medical School conducting full time medical research funded by the Wellcome Trust authoring research publications principally on the role of the pituitary hormones ACTH and endorphin in pregnancy and parturition, and the pineal hormone melatonin in growth and puberty. Post retirement (from medicine) a theatre producer introducing Joan Rivers at the Edinburgh Festival then taking her into the West End of London (Theatre Royal Haymarket) and on a UK and Ireland tour. He has also produced Off-West End and at the Steppenwolf Theatre in Chicago, and the Beckett Theatre in New York. He has two patents granted by the US Patent and Trademark Office, "A Quality Filter for the Internet" (Patent: 7895202) and "Rewards for Unseen Website Activity" (Patent: 8311881). Recently founder of Doctors Club, **https://www.doctorsclubuk.com** , a sort of internet co-op.

www.ingramcontent.com/pod-product-compliance
Lightning Source LLC
Chambersburg PA
CBHW051156220526
45473CB00003B/794